ALREADY CHOSEN

Loving Your Life in the Midst of Longing

JESSICA MATHISEN

JESSICA MATHISEN

www.jessicanmathisen.com

Copyright © 2018 Jessica Mathisen

First printing, 2018

Cover design by: Shelby Nickel

Scripture unless otherwise noted, is taken from the Holy Bible, English Standard Version, Copyright 2001 by Crossway, a publishing ministry of Good News Publishers.

© Jessica Mathisen

ALREADY CHOSEN

To all of my sweet friends in the midst of longing, may you know the love of your Heavenly Father and His delight in you.

Table of Contents

Introduction

Marriage. For many Christians, this is the ultimate goal and the place in which all of our hopes and dreams will be satisfied. It is in Christian marriage and the subsequent privilege of raising a Christian family that we believe all of our hopes are fulfilled. So many men and women yearn for marriage and long to have their perfect fairy tale dreams come true. But what happens when you're twenty-six or thirty-six or forty-six, and you're still single? What happens when you are the last of your friends to walk down the aisle and you feel like the third wheel in nearly every social situation? Is there something wrong with you? Did you do something to jeopardize your opportunity for true love? Are you to be pitied?

Friend, in our society and within Christian culture, there is so much value placed on love, marriage, and family, and there is nothing wrong with that! But feeling as though you are doing something wrong or being ignored because you do not have a mate can get old quickly. How do you sort through the feelings that sometimes overwhelm you? Is it acceptable to feel this way? What if you can no longer see a light at the end of this seemingly never-ending tunnel?

Here is the good news, friend. God has not forsaken you. He has not left you or abandoned you. In fact, if you are in Christ, He is right by your side. You have nothing to fear. You don't have to scramble to try to figure it all out. He's got you. Even if you've never been asked out on a date, He's already chosen you. He's already spoken joy and fulfillment over your life, regardless of your marital status. He loves you exactly for who you are, because He created you. There is nothing tricky about it, and there is nothing you have to do to make sure He never leaves. Will you choose to believe it?

As someone who was always the bridesmaid and was a bit of a late bloomer in the dating realm, I want to share with you all God has shown me on this crazy journey. It took me a long time to learn that what He says is what matters most. When you live like you're already chosen, your joy and trust are in Him, and you won't be shaken, because He's got you. I pray my story encourages you to live in your now and to not be afraid of what may or may not come. He has chosen you, and that is all that matters.

ALREADY CHOSEN

Chapter 1

Dreaming of Love

A dream is a wish your heart makes, when you're fast asleep.
In dreams, you will lose your heartaches.
Whatever you wish for, you keep.
- Cinderella

"I now pronounce you husband and wife. You may kiss the bride." These are the words I could not wait to hear on my wedding day. It turns out I did not have to wait long, because these words (or something like them) were said to me on the playground in third grade. My third-grade steady boyfriend, Benjamin, and I were getting married, and I couldn't have been happier. We had been together for almost all of third grade, so things were pretty serious. My mom and dad recall seeing us holding hands on science night as we walked down our elementary school hallway. What more could an eight-year-old ask for? All my dreams had come true.

Elementary school is not a time when most people have their eyes peeled for their future spouse, but I was not like most people. Even as a child, I longed for marriage. I loved to play house and to think about what it would be like to one day have a family of my own. I was three years old when my younger sister Lauren was born. My parents gave me a baby doll so I could practice holding the baby before my sister's arrival. I loved my baby doll and loved my sister. It was then that the desire to be a mama was planted in my heart. Later on, as I began to daydream and find myself in the stories of Disney princesses, I knew I wanted to find my Prince Charming. Everything would be perfect when I was "rescued" by my knight in shining armor!

Now let me be clear. I had a pretty normal childhood with a happy home life. There were bumps and bruises along the way, just like everyone experiences. However, my expansive knowledge of fairy tales led me to believe that my world would be set in motion when I met my prince. As the older sibling, I fit my stereotype quite well. I was organized, high-achieving, and a people pleaser. I liked making others happy and thrived in environments where I was praised and adored (read: where I was the center of attention). But there were many times where I was not popular or cool. Even in elementary school, I experienced the sting of rejection a few times, and it influenced the way I related to others as a result. When you are attempting to perform in an effort to earn others' love, you tire of feeling like you do not measure up. So, when the rejection came in various forms, I would usually try to change my personality in an effort to win people over. You want me to be funny? I'm your girl! Oh, you like it when I make fun of others and laugh at their expense? Count me in! Much of my time was spent attempting to appease my peers, whose acceptance I so badly longed for.

In elementary school, I was a social butterfly, always talking and trying to get to know my peers. I wanted to be liked and noticed by everyone and found attention to be a great source of affirmation. However, I did not know what it meant to be known. When I look back, I think even at that tender age, I actually wanted to be known intimately. But what elementary aged child can articulate that deep, heartfelt need? My actions demonstrated otherwise - I simply wanted people to know my name and want to be my friend. My family moved around a couple times within my elementary school years, and it was extremely difficult for me to handle the process of transitioning to a new house, school, and church. Even though I was very young at the time, I can still remember our moves being quite traumatic. I liked the comfort of the familiar and did not want to imagine a different life. My sister and I were both born in Nashville, Tennessee, and then we moved to Indianapolis, Indiana (where my third-grade boyfriend and I were wed, of course), and three years later, we moved to Marietta, Georgia.

When we moved to Marietta, I was nine years old, and I remember being nervous as I wondered if I would like the new kids at my school and whether or not I would get along well with my teacher. Elementary school kids can be vicious! What if I did not wear the right clothes or say the right things? In Indianapolis, I had been in the "advanced reading group" and was pretty near the top of my class (or at least that's what I like to think; I don't have any real data to back that up). But in Marietta, I was suddenly surrounded by kids who were smarter than me. Imagine that! I was no longer the top of the class. I did not have my little third grade boyfriend anymore, and making friends proved to more difficult than it had been in the past. Everything had changed, and I was just "the new girl." I greatly struggled with peer relationships, and I wanted so badly to be liked for who I was. The problem was, I wasn't even sure who I was. Since I was constantly trying to secure others' approval, I did not know who to be in order to find "my people." However, I found myself constantly trying to be like everyone around me in order to gain acceptance. They say that imitation is the sincerest form of flattery, and boy, did I know how to flatter others.

Fast forward to middle school, a time you absolutely could not pay me enough money to return to. In middle school, I was flat out boy crazy. Hormones were raging and boys were pretty cute, so who didn't dream of their favorite boy band crush or their pre-algebra classmate? (Side note: I still love Justin Timberlake and am not ashamed of it). The problem for me in middle school was that I was all kinds of nerdy. There was just no way around it. I had big glasses, was always just behind the curve with fashion, and tried way too hard.

I had so many crushes, and so much mental energy and time was wasted on dreaming about boys who probably did not know my name. It was super cool to have a boyfriend, so while I "went out with" a boy from church, we never went anywhere and maybe talked on the phone three times. And you know what? I asked him out because my friend dared me to. I knew he liked me and figured I might as well do something about it. Not my best moment.

Middle school was just a whole lot of awkward for me, as I'm sure it was for you, too. Anyone who skips the awkward phase has to have it coming for them at some point! Even if you were part of the illustrious "popular crowd," I'm sure you can think of a few situations you wish could be erased from your history. As a child, I was never part of a sports team. I loved to read and participated in a year of ballet, but other than that, sports were not part of my repertoire. Field day was always something I looked forward to because we didn't have school work, but I also dreaded it because my athletic abilities were subpar at best. I remember one such day so clearly — we were doing a relay race, and I didn't really understand the rules. I ran to tag the person who was next, who just happened to be one of the most popular (and of course, attractive) boys in school. In my hurry and in my dizziness, I tripped and fell right at his feet. I practically groped him as I reached up to tag him, and he very nonchalantly looked down at me and then turned away quickly, like I wasn't even there. I felt pretty small.

In middle school, I wanted to hold hands with someone, to talk to someone and be understood. Basically, I wanted a boyfriend, and I wanted one badly! It was bad enough that I was a nerd, but it was also tough to see friends around me "go out" (that's "go steady" for you old school folks) with their little dreamboats and feel like that just might not ever happen for me. I was only 13 years old, and already I was feeling desperate about my lack of a love life! I sure did need some perspective! Looking back at my middle school phase, I would tell myself to chill out and just have fun getting to know my friends. I would tell myself to stand strong in who I was made to be in Christ and not to feel like I had to do things just because other kids my age were doing them. I would tell myself to hang out with my little sister more and enjoy getting to know her. I would also tell myself to give my parents a break. But you know what they say, my friend. Hindsight is 20/20.

No one meets their future husband in high school anyways. These were my thoughts as I considered what my dating life should look like in high school. I was fortunate enough to grow up in a wonderful church with a solid youth group. In middle school, I learned what it meant to have a growing and thriving relationship with God by spending time in His word. In high school, I continued this discipline by spending time reading my Bible and truly getting to know Him by understanding His truths and how He wanted me to apply them to my life.

My youth pastor was an incredible man who encouraged us to dig deep and become who were made to be in Christ. He allowed us the opportunity to grow and was never afraid of or shocked by any of our questions. I grew up in the "True Love Waits" era, which means that many Christian teens and young adults wore rings and made pledges to save sex for marriage, as God intended for it to be. I remember a Wednesday night sermon series entitled "Love, Sex, and Starbucks" at our church that was centered around the Bible's standards for love, dating, and marriage. While most kids were easily excited at the prospect of dating and wanted to be well-liked, the majority certainly weren't thinking about marriage.

During this time, my philosophy on dating was heavily influenced by my thoughts about the future. I wondered if I began dating someone in high school whether or not that person would matter to me in 10 years. Would we even be friends? If marriage was my end goal, would dating in high school actually help me meet that goal? When I considered these questions, I realized that for most people, they don't meet their future spouse in high school. I believed high school to be a time when I needed to focus on my schoolwork so I could be accepted to the best college possible, so I made the decision to not date until I went to college. Now, when I say that I "made the decision," you have to understand that there were not a ton of propositions I was refusing, so it was not a huge sacrifice on my part at the time. But it was my way of saying to the Lord, "I'm Yours. This life isn't my own. I trust You with the results."

While it was a semi-scary thing for me to say that I wouldn't date in high school, it was most assuredly the best thing for me at that time. There is no way I had the emotional maturity to maintain any sort of "relationship" at that point. On the outside, I looked as though I had it all together — I made good grades, stayed out of trouble, and attended church regularly. But I was so wrapped up in fairy tales and sweet dreams that I don't know how I would have handled a relationship at this stage in my life. When I look back, I can see how God protected me from so much. There were friends of mine who dated and had their hearts broken. And while I was longing for someone to hold, I was glad to be spared of the heartache that inevitably accompanies a relationship that goes beyond the platonic stage.

Here's the thing, though: although I chose not to date, I was still heavily invested in my lack of a love life mentally. I still continued my boy crazy ways from middle school, and I often daydreamed about boys who were friends or acquaintances or even classmates who barely knew I existed. As an avid reader and one who loves to immerse herself in a good story, I often looked to books and movies to inform my thoughts about what dating would be like "when I finally got there." Most of these books and movies I read had little to no basis in reality. Thus, I still found myself highly emotionally involved in friendships with guys who most assuredly weren't my boyfriends, but I loved being "just friends" with. Does that make sense? I was not dating "officially," but I had "friends" that I was quite fond of, and in my mind, we might as well have been dating. That, my friends, is called "stinkin' thinkin'." We'll get to more of that a little later.

Overall, high school was a pleasant experience for me. I made it out relatively unscathed and was able to leave without a ton of regrets. At this point, you could still classify me as a nerd, although I would never have admitted it at the time. But I was disciplined in my schoolwork and tried to be kind to the people around me. And while I had the normal teenage tussles with my parents (as most kids do), I didn't sneak out, do drugs, or drink alcohol. I made good grades, played the violin, sang in the praise team at church, and was involved in various clubs and honor societies. On paper, I was looking pretty dang good. However, I was still very naive and didn't really know what "the cool kids" were doing. There were so many things about the world I had yet to understand and discover. One thing I knew for sure was that I had worked my butt off for four years to get to the University of Georgia, and I couldn't wait to be there.

Chapter 2

Yearning for Love

Hope deferred makes the heart sick, but a desire fulfilled is a tree of life. - Proverbs 13:12

When I entered my freshman year at the University of Georgia, I more or less thought, "Where are all the boys? Bring them to me!" I expected that because I had "given up" dating in high school (and remember, I didn't really have to scare the men off), college was my fresh start to meet Mr. Right. I had the perfect plan prepared in my mind. Somehow, someway, somewhere, I would meet him, and we'd date all through the college years, get married, and start having some babies.

The first semester of college was a huge reality check for me. I had a "potluck" (random) roommate whom I had never met, and our personalities didn't quite mesh (That's putting it nicely). Before leaving for school, I remember being extremely excited about everything my college days would hold for me. I figured I would make a ton of new friends, hang out with them all the time, and meet the man of my dreams. But that first semester, I quickly found out that making friends has to be an intentional act, and finding true friends takes time. I deeply missed my friends from home, and I missed my family. Before I left for school, I was very prideful and thought I would not really want to talk to my family much; I was glad for my newfound freedom! But I found myself calling home quite often in order to process all of the new experiences being thrust at me each day. My social life wasn't quite what I thought it would be. Many nights were spent in my dorm just watching movies by myself because I struggled with finding a way to initiate plans. I began to understand just how much I had taken for granted within the comforts of home.

It was in my college years where I really found my footing, as I was on my path to self-discovery. I began to understand my strengths and weaknesses more and even found some new passions! The Baptist Collegiate Ministries on campus was where I met some amazing girls who are still my best friends today. After a rocky first semester, I was finally able to find community with these friends and began hanging out with them regularly. My first couple years at school, I loved my growing group of friends. I was a social butterfly and enjoyed going to events, dancing and singing loudly, and laughing obnoxiously in the dining hall.

Until college, I led quite the sheltered life and I was very uncomfortable around alcohol. I didn't know much about the Greek life of fraternities and sororities and was terrified of frat parties. My entire perception of college parties was informed by movies and television, as I'd never gone to any "real" parties when I was in high school. When I was invited to a frat party, I was in turmoil wondering whether or not I should attend, and after a few hours of going back and forth, I realized that my discomfort at the thought probably gave me a good reason to stay behind. Making decisions on my own like that was something altogether new for me. I wanted to stay true to who I was, but looking back, I feel some of my decisions were rooted in fear - fear of the unknown and fear of judgment. The Lord began to teach me more about what it meant to truly live out my faith, and I discovered what it meant to follow Him. I realized that as an ambassador for Christ, my life really did have to look different than those around me. He also showed me that I could make a difference just by being myself. People truly were watching me and wanted to know the reasoning behind the decisions I made.

I still took my studies seriously, but my boy-crazy ways from middle and high school had not stopped. I had multiple crushes, and usually there was at least one guy that I fantasized about constantly. As I moved through the years at school, a lot of my friends were still single, but that number was beginning to decrease. My major was Early Childhood Education, so most of my classes during my junior and senior year were female dominated. In the South, some people call this degree an "M.R.S. degree," which means you're going to college just to have a degree on hand that you may or may not need — your Plan A is to get married! But how was I going to meet someone if I was always around girls? It became clear to me that my plan of marrying my college sweetheart was obviously not going to come to fruition.

When I graduated from UGA in May 2010, I was a bridesmaid in a wedding the following month, and I also had invitations to two others on the same day. At this point, the wedding fever had only just begun. I've lost count, but I'm sure I attended at least 20, maybe 30 weddings before my own. My dream was to get married after graduating, or at least be dating someone during my senior year who I would eventually marry. But there was no one knocking at my door or calling me on the phone who could have fulfilled these dreams.

During these years, I read all the "right books" and did all the "right things" a good single Christian girl should do. I was highly involved in my campus ministry and church. I didn't cuss, and at that point I believed you couldn't be a Christian and drink alcohol, so that wasn't a part of my lifestyle either. So, what was I doing wrong?

In this time of waiting, I certainly was doing a lot of "the right things," but when it came down to it, I wasn't doing all the right things. Because after all, when are we really doing all the right things? At this point in my life, I was in my early twenties, and I was desperate for some attention. I was beginning to think that something was wrong with me. Was I not saying the right things or wearing the right clothes? Was I too forward or too shy? Was I too smart or not smart enough? I had been on a few dates, but nothing lasting had come out of those experiences. I was twenty-two years old and felt as though I were destined to be an old maid as I watched friend after friend walk down the aisle to her happily ever after.

This season in my life was marked by many "pseudo-relationships." You know the drill. Boy meets girl. Girl likes boy. Boy flirts with girl. Boy texts girl. Boy may even call girl on the phone. Boy "hangs out" with girl. But boy never pursues girl. Girl sits around waiting and wishing and hoping that one day boy will "wake up" and see how amazing she is and that they will ride off into the sunset together, hand in hand, longingly gazing into each other's eyes. (Think Taylor Swift's song "You Belong with Me"). Boy gets tired of/bored with girl. Boy stops paying attention to girl. Girl is confused, lonely, and heartbroken. Girl moves on to repeat the process with another boy, hoping that he will be different from the last one.

It is so much easier to settle for less when you are yearning for something that seems unattainable, isn't it? When I was involved in my "pseudo-relationships," I often rationalized my behavior. Looking back, I think deep down I knew these guys were not 100% right for me. But I wanted attention and affection so badly that I was willing to give pieces of myself away without getting much back in return.

Sadly, this was a game I knew well, and it was a cycle I allowed for far too long. I so deeply desired something, anything, to work, to click, for it to be magical like all of the romantic comedies I had watched over the years. But it never did. And in my desperation, impatience, and immaturity, I ended up giving many little pieces of my heart away, never to see them returned or validated. Remember how I said earlier that there was always someone I was fantasizing about? Well, I used to think these little fantasies were harmless. But it turns out they are downright detrimental to my emotional and mental well-being. How could I claim the name of Christ and settle for so much less?

During this season, I often settled for less than, (the "cheap substitute") if you will, and my heart suffered for it. One of my favorite Bible stories is in John 4, where Jesus meets the Samaritan woman at the well. This story has captivated my heart for many years. In this story, a Samaritan woman has gone to the well to draw water in midday. To us modern readers, there isn't much cause for suspicion when we read this text, but if you look at the historical context of this story, we find that this behavior would have been quite strange. However, the choice to draw from the well at midday was deliberate on her part. The Samaritans and the Jews were not friendly toward one another, in fact, they were extremely antagonistic. Sadly, this woman had an unfavorable reputation. For her to come in the middle of the day to draw water from the well was an intentional choice that would isolate her and enable her to avoid social interaction and judgement.

But friend, Jesus knew her heart and her story of rebellion, rejection, and abandonment. He saw her longing for a love that is deep and wild and unfailing. In fact, because He is sovereign and omniscient, He went out of His way to stop at the well, just to have a life-changing conversation with this dear woman. And when He talked with her, He began to tell her exactly what He saw. Let's look at it together:

A woman from Samaria came to draw water. Jesus said to her, "Give me a drink." (For his disciples had gone away into the city to buy food.) The Samaritan woman said to him, "How is it that you, a Jew, ask for a drink from me, a woman of Samaria?" (For Jews have no dealings with Samaritans.) Jesus answered her, "If you knew the gift of God, and who it is that is saying to you, 'Give me a drink" you would have asked him, and he would have given you living water." The woman said to him, "Sir, you have nothing to draw water with, and the well is deep. Where do you get that living water? Are you greater than our father Jacob? He gave us the well and drank from it himself, as did his sons and his livestock." Jesus said to her, "Everyone who drinks of this water will be thirsty again, but whoever drinks of the water that I will give him will never be thirsty again. The water that I will give him will become in him a spring of water welling up to eternal life." The woman said to him, "Sir, give me this water, so that I will not be thirsty or have to come here to draw water."

Jesus said to her, "Go, call your husband, and come here." The woman answered him, "I have no husband." Jesus said to her, "You are right in saying, 'I have no husband'; for you have had five husbands, and the one you now have is not your husband. What you have said is true." The woman said to him, "Sir, I perceive that you are a prophet. Our fathers worshiped on this mountain, but you say that in Jerusalem is the place where people ought to worship." Jesus said to her, "Woman, believe me, the hour is coming when neither on this mountain nor in Jerusalem will you worship the Father. You worship what you do not know; we worship what we know, for salvation is from the Jews. But the hour is coming, and is now here, when the true worshipers will worship the Father in spirit and truth, for the Father is seeking such people to worship him. God is spirit, and those who worship him must worship in spirit and truth." The woman said to him, "I know that Messiah is coming (he who is called Christ). When he

*comes, he will tell us all things." Jesus said to her, "I who
speak to you am he."*
- *John 4:7-20*

Jesus does three things here: He calls her to accountability,
He gently corrects her, and He leads her to a better way. When
Jesus meets this woman, He is quick to let her know that He is
aware of her lifestyle, and He wants more for her, because He
longs to give immeasurably more than all that we ask or imagine
(Ephesians 3:20). It's just who He is. Jesus does not ignore the
status of her heart or dance around her sin. He steps right into her
life and says, "Beloved, you're making choices that are going to
hurt you, and if you don't stop, you will continue to be hurt. You
were made for more. You were made for Me." He does not suggest
a 10-step program or a change of scenery, but rather Himself,
knowing that He is the only One who can satisfy her deepest needs
and longings. The Samaritan woman is completely undone by His
grace, mercy, and tenderness, and in the following verses, she
leaves everything behind and tells the townspeople about the
encounter she just experienced with the one true Son of God.
When the Samaritan woman encountered Jesus face to face,
everything changed. All of the cheap substitutes she'd been
chasing in an attempt to fill the emptiness within were suddenly
devoid of any value or meaning. She had seen Jesus, she had
tasted of His living water, and she wanted more.

How often do we ask Jesus for something we want and
then run around trying to force ourselves into happiness when He
does not deliver when, or how, we want Him to? How often do we
believe that we deserve something because "everyone else" has it
and we desperately do not want to feel left out or less than? How
often do we ask for the wrong reasons and expect to be blessed
anyways? How often do we act out of our insecurities instead of
from our secure identity in Christ Jesus, our Cornerstone who
never, ever changes or casts a shifting shadow?

When we attempt to get what we believe we deserve by
settling for a lesser way, we are robbing ourselves of the abundant
life that Jesus has promised for us in John 10:10. We are
corroborating with the enemy of our souls and advancing his plan
for destruction by accepting far less than the riches Jesus has for
us. Jesus offers us the best of the best. He spares us nothing that

He knows would bless us, and yet in our immaturity and impatience, we neglect to see what He has done by focusing on what He has yet to give us.

C.S. Lewis writes in *The Weight of Glory*:

> *It would seem that our Lord finds our desires not too strong, but too weak. We are half-hearted creatures, fooling about with drink and sex and ambition when infinite joy is offered us, like an ignorant child who wants to go on making mud pies in a slum because he cannot imagine what is meant by the offer of a holiday at the sea. We are far too easily pleased.*[1]

Have you settled for the mud pies before, friend? Are there times where you have questioned God's goodness because He has yet to fulfill a dream within your heart? Are you consumed by this dream and obsessed with making it a reality in your life? When I was in the midst of my "pseudo-relationships," the answer to all of these questions was a resounding "yes." I settled, I questioned God's goodness, and I was consumed with the dream of romantic love becoming a reality in my life. What I didn't do was look around at the life I'd been given, which was already pretty dang good. No, I wasn't married, but my life was still full and beautiful. I had a great group of friends, a wonderful church, and a family who was supportive of me regardless of my marital status. I had hobbies and passions and dreams beyond marriage. So why did I think that a man would fix everything?

When I was looking for a man to change my world and fix everything that I thought was wrong, my hopes were in the wrong places. I worshiped the dream instead of the Dream Giver. I wanted what other people had, and I was afraid of a life that looked different than the "perfect" one I had constructed in my mind. Friend, when I was constantly fantasizing about my guy "friends" with whom I was in pseudo-relationships, I was settling for the cheap substitute. I was far too easily pleased. I allowed my imagination to carry me to places it really didn't need to go — dates that never really happened, kisses that were not real, and wedding ceremonies that were nothing but a wish and a dream. I was so busy trying to fabricate what I believed would fill me up that I wasn't allowing God Himself to be my portion, my strength, and my joy. And when you're living out of a place of desperation, the actions that follow often are not the ones you're the proudest of.

Chapter 3

Desperate for Love

There is a way that seems right to a man, but its end is the way to death. - Proverbs 16:25

Here's the danger with giving your heart away too soon —
it gets broken and then broken again. The pain I experienced as I
watched several friends pair off with a significant other was
genuine. Proverbs tell us that "hope deferred makes the heart sick"
(Proverbs 13:12, ESV). And friends, I was definitely heartsick. My
mind would go to "worst case scenario" mode — forever singleness
— often. And I didn't want to be forever single. I wanted the
flowers, the hand-holding, and the diamond ring. I wanted to
believe that I was special and worth pursuing and fighting for. But
instead of clinging to the promises of God to sustain and
strengthen me, I settled.

The "pseudo-relationships" I allowed myself to be a part of
were so very damaging to my heart. It took months, and even
years, after each subsequent "breakup" to process and move
forward. There was so much mental and emotional energy poured
into these relationships, because I believed that at some point he
might choose me instead of the other girl he was interested in (or
the girl he was currently dating). As I watched so many friends
walk down the aisle to a new beginning, it became increasingly
difficult for me to not manipulate my situations to find a way to
feel valued and chosen.

I'll let you in on a very embarrassing story here, friends. It's
a tale of how I tried to manipulate my circumstances in order to
force a relationship into existence. There was this one guy I kept
coming back to in my mind over the course of several years. (Yep,
you read that right. Years. I don't give up without a fight.) We had

several mutual friends (and when I say several, I mean like, hundreds on Facebook) and we seemed to like all the same things. He was tall, dark, and handsome. Plus, he was a believer! I mean, how can you get any better than that? If we dated, we would have all the same friends and do all the same things we already did, just together! I figured it was a win-win. We were headed for a life of love and happiness, he just didn't know it yet. Clearly, it was up to me to get his attention. We had met briefly a few times through some of our mutual friends, and I just knew we were destined to be together. So what did I do, you ask? I stalked him. And y'all, I'm not talking about Facebook stalking here. Facebook was only the means of my intel. I saw he made plans with someone to be at a particular coffee shop in town one afternoon, and you better believe I "just happened" to find myself there, too. We talked for maybe 30 seconds, and nothing came of it. And when I say nothing, I truly mean nothing. We didn't "hang out," and we certainly didn't go on a date. But I was convinced he just needed time to see the depths of my amazingness. Smooth, right? Y'all. I was a legit crazy person. God bless this hot mess.

Do you see the danger here, my friend? When we choose to let someone or something else (or the idea of someone or something else) give us comfort and define our worth, we're replacing God. We're idolaters, in every sense of the word. We've decided that a stamp of approval or a fleeting moment of pleasure is worth more than what the Creator of the universe says about us. Why do we believe what someone else thinks, says, or does to us is more valuable than the approval of our Heavenly Father? Why would we put our hopes in man alone? God says our hope must be built on Him, or it is surely going to shift and sink when the pressures of this life come. When we build everything around a dream or a person, we are setting ourselves up for complete failure.

I used to think, "Well, as long as I get married before Jesus comes back, I'll be good. Then I will have really lived." I cannot even begin to tell you all of the things that are wrong with this way of thinking. This line of thinking is completely and totally wrapped up in the here and now. But the truth is, I was not made for this day alone. I was created for eternity, and my goal must be to live with this in mind. In fact, His word says that His ways are higher than ours (Isaiah 55:8-9). If His ways are so different than our own, then why do we continually try to outsmart Him or bring Him our "perfect" life plan? God's perspective is completely different than ours, because He not only knows the past, He knows the future. God is eternal. The book of Revelation refers to Him as the Alpha and Omega, which is the beginning and the end. He was, is, and is to come. He can see the whole picture. And because He can see the whole picture, He fully understands that our lives are but a little blip on the map of eternity. I don't even know for sure what will happen 30 minutes from now, yet I somehow have convinced myself on numerous occasions that I know a better plan for my entire life than He does! I allow myself to be consumed with what I can see right in front of me instead of fixing my eyes on what is unseen and eternal. Does this sound familiar to anyone, or am I alone here?

Keep your heart with all vigilance, for from it flow the springs of life. (ESV)

Be careful what you think, because your thoughts run your life. (NCV)
- Proverbs 4:2

We often hear this verse in conjunction with talks about dating and relationships. But what does it mean? How in the world are you supposed to guard your heart? What does that even look like? Does it only apply to dating, or can it be applied to the Christian life in general?

Your heart is the center of who you are. It's what makes you uniquely you. It's your innermost thoughts, feelings, fears, and dreams. In my singleness, my heart was characterized by fear and insecurity rooted in my lack of a significant other. I wanted to be loved. I didn't want to be the last one to be chosen, or worse, never chosen at all. I didn't want to be single forever. I thought that all of my problems wouldn't be as bad, or would straight up disappear, once I met the man of my dreams. Boy was I wrong. More on this later.

In *Heart Made Whole*, Christa Black Gifford writes:

> *This inner realm — the center of your being — is*
> *the origin of every move you make, every word you speak,*

every thought you think, and every action you take.
Plainly put, your insides produce your outsides. You are
the landlord of your heart, and you control who takes up
residence. When God moved into your life, you didn't sign
over ownership papers to your building where He took
control. Rather, He gave you possession of your heart
long ago and will never take back that gift... He needs you
to give Him access to every floor, every room, and every
locked, forgotten space.[1]

My heart was given to me by God Himself. He shaped me, formed me, and spoke life into me. When I became a daughter of His, He gave me His name and a new identity. But I wasn't walking in that identity. I may have believed He chose me to be His "good Christian girl," but I didn't walk in my identity as a royal daughter of the King. I wanted someone to validate me in the flesh. I wanted to know I was worth choosing and pursuing. His love for me wasn't enough because I wasn't consumed by Him. Instead, I was consumed by my desires, dreams, and wishes.

Your heart, too, is sacred and precious. It is the center of who you are and is to be guarded, not in self-preservation, but with wisdom and discernment for who can enter into your secret places. When I decided to settle and play around with relationships, I was not guarding my heart. I was allowing these men who gave me no promise or any kind of intention into my heart because I wanted to be loved and given attention in the worst way. I shared my life with them and told them of my dreams and passions, because I hoped and expected for their reciprocation to be in the form of a romantic relationship. Instead, I got half-hearted texts (sometimes) and sporadic fun hang-outs. No dates. No wining and dining. No true pursuit. But I fell hard and fast, and I didn't allow myself to look to the Lord to be my everything. I wanted to be wrapped up in someone else's world and looked to these "pseudo-relationships" to fulfill needs which could only be fulfilled by Christ Himself.

God does not want us to be consumed with our desires, dreams, and wishes. He wants us to be consumed by Him. He wants our love for Him to burn white hot in our souls, just barely able to be contained. He wants us to be on fire for Him, walking

18

with Him, and trusting that He will indeed provide and meet our every need in His timing. What I could not come to grips with in this season was the thought that a husband was actually not a need, but a want. We were all made for community and intimate relationships. The Christian life is not meant to be lived in isolation. And while God Himself said in Genesis 2 that it is not good for man to be alone, He didn't attach a promise of marriage for everyone to that statement.

Well-meaning friends can say the absolute worst things to you at this time, too, am I right?

"When you are happy with where you are, then God can bring him to you."
"God wouldn't give you the desire if He wasn't going to fulfill it."
"It's all about His timing."
"Have you tried online dating?"
"I have a friend who was just like you, but she did x, y, z, and now she's married."
"Make sure you just enjoy this time. Sometimes I wish I still had the freedom you have!"

If you are married and reading this **DO NOT SAY THESE THINGS TO YOUR SINGLE FRIENDS**. Just trust me on this one. Just enter into their hurt with them. Give wisdom when it's solicited, but don't feel like because you are married you have all the answers. And single friends, do not allow bitterness to creep into your heart when your married friends are trying their best to encourage you. I can remember when one of my friends told me, "It's just all about God's timing," and I literally wanted to scream. I thought to myself, "Well of course you can say that. You're married and you've got your happily ever after. I'm still binge-watching Netflix in bed all by myself!"

There is a danger that every believer faces when a desire becomes a demand. We like to quote Psalm 37:4, which says, "Delight yourself in the Lord, and he will give you the desires of your heart." But the reality is that there is an unspoken expectation lurking behind our commitment to delight in the Lord — we think we have a conditional relationship with Him. We read it as an "If, then" statement and believe that if we do the right things, then He will give us what we want. It's classic positive reinforcement. We say to ourselves, sometimes unknowingly, "God, if I do all the right things for You, then You will give me what I want." We treat God like Santa Claus, and when we receive what we deem to be a lump of coal when we thought were not on the nice list, we are very disappointed indeed.

This verse actually means that when we delight in the Lord, our desires will begin to change and mold into something different altogether. A heart that delights in the Lord is stirred by Him. This heart is moved by His ways and His word. This heart longs to be more like Jesus and draw nearer to the Father by the help of the Holy Spirit in every moment of every day. The heart that delights in the Lord is most delighted and enraptured by Him, and its sole aim is to know Him and to make Him known. Thus, this heart is satisfied in Him alone, with no need of anything else to satiate its appetite. John Piper says, "God is most glorified in us when we are most satisfied in Him." If my aim is to know God and to make Him known, my marital status does not matter. It has no bearing on my effectiveness in the Kingdom of God, and it certainly does not change my worth as a daughter of the Most High King.

Your marital status does not define you. Let me say that again a little slower for you. Your. marital. status. does. not. define. you. I know when we introduce ourselves in a group, our jobs and marital status are the information we lead with, but they are not what define us. We are more than a job and we are more than an attachment to a significant other. We are chosen by God, loved by Him, and made to know Him. This is truly the only thing that matters and the only thing that should define our lives — our standing with Christ.

Here's the thing: God does not owe me anything. He just doesn't. His love for me is more than enough. Everything else He decides to give me out of His wonderful generosity is just icing on the cake. And the same is true for you, my friend. Romans 5:8 says, "but God shows his love for us in that while we were still sinners, Christ died for us." God sent His only Son for me. He died a sinner's death on a cross, stretched out His arms, hung His head and said, "It is finished." He trampled death and defeated the grave, and yet in my singleness, I had the nerve to believe He wasn't enough. I thought I needed someone else to make me happy and to make my dreams come true. My perspective was so very wrong, and yet it is a common one I see in so many today who are not living out the dream they imagined for themselves.

How do we get to the point where we have demands that we are begging God to fulfill? I often had a "victim mentality" in my singleness. I was the self-proclaimed victim of my circumstances, the poor single girl who was alone and lonely. How's that for depressing? Boy, was I negative! But the truth was that I had a great life. My family was supportive and loving, and I had friends in various circles and fun hobbies. And um, I had Jesus. He's kind of the best. As a "chronically single" person, I often felt like I deserved certain things, which is why I was desperate to do what I "had" to do to get what I wanted. I wanted to manipulate and control every little thing in order to ensure that my happy ending came. But when does God reward us for trying to do everything on our own? (Spoiler alert: never.)

Now friend, I enjoy a good love story with the best of them. But my life was not a picture-perfect love story, and all of my attempts at manipulation to craft such a life (the coffee shop, albeit extreme, was just one example) were not working. So, on those lonely nights when I wasn't asked to join anyone for dinner and a movie, I would often curl up with a good book or a watch yet another chick flick. Duh. I'm not saying that there is anything wrong with reading or watching movies. But there is something wrong when you allow these carefully crafted and scripted stories to inform your expectations for reality. And this is exactly what I did. I did not have my own real-life love story, so I escaped into the stories of others and imagined that I was a part of them. I would then fantasize about my own story playing out just like these nearly memorized stories — a tale of beauty, not too much struggle, and the happiest ending you ever did see. Have you ever done the same? Have you allowed yourself to get so lost and enraptured in a story that wasn't your own that you forgot to live well the life that is right in front of you? No matter the season, we must keep our eyes on Christ, friend!

During this season, I was reading my Bible, going to church, and attending Bible study, but I did not always cling to God's truth as though it truly had the power to not only save my life but change my heart and mind. When I hopped on Facebook and saw yet another engagement, my heart was not full of joy. It was full of bitterness, questioning, and longing. And while it is embarrassing to admit it, I often felt sorry for myself when I continually saw others' lives seem to move on without me. Surely there was a better way, and I wanted to find it.

Chapter 4

Sowing Seeds

Those who plant in tears will harvest with shouts of joy. They weep as they go to plant their seed, but they sing as they return with the harvest. - Psalm 126:5-6 (NLT)

After I graduated from the University of Georgia, I moved to Chihuahua, Mexico and lived there for two years. I travelled to Mexico on a mission trip when I was 15, and the Holy Spirit told me then that I was going to come back one day. Fast forward seven years later, and my dreams were coming true. I went to Mexico not knowing a single soul with full bags and a willing heart. I had the amazing opportunity to work as an elementary teacher at the school for missionaries' kids. When I moved to Mexico, it was truly a new beginning. While I had moved around in my life, never before had I completely started over in a place so far away from literally everyone I knew, and I certainly had never done it on my own. When I didn't have a "ring by spring" at UGA, I wondered if I might meet someone in Mexico. But I also knew I wasn't there to meet a man; I was there to serve Jesus and know Him more (but I still secretly desired to marry a Mexican man. Just keeping it real).

My time in Mexico was so good for my heart. It was there where I learned that God was always with me and that He would never ever leave or forsake me. I had known this for years in my head, but in Chihuahua, this head knowledge became heart knowledge. While I lived in Mexico, I was the youngest person on the mission field. I was fresh out of school and ready for adventure, but I was also very lonely. It turns out that living in another country on your own (or at all) can be extremely emotionally trying at times. But it was through my times of loneliness where I learned to cry out to God and give Him all of my thoughts, fears, worries, concerns, and dreams. And because He is God and He is faithful, He continued to mold and shape me.

The first year in Mexico, I lived with a roommate who was Mexican-American. I like to say she had the best of both worlds. We lived in a cute little yellow house we affectionately named La Casita Amarilla. She was able to help me form relationships by always inviting her Mexican friends over to our house, which helped me take my Spanish to another level. Her friends became my friends, and pretty soon our little "crew" was inseparable. We hosted game nights and went to dinner and threw parties and just had way too much fun. During my first year, I experienced another "pseudo-relationship" where I pulled out all the stops in hopes that this "friend" would recognize he was head over heels in love with me. You can guess how it turned out.

While it took some time for me to acclimate and acquire a friend group, transitioning to life in another country was quite difficult. I studied Spanish from middle school all the way through college, but living in a foreign country and having to make another language your primary means of communication is altogether different than writing a paper or having a conversation in class with another non-native speaker. I visited several churches and was often discouraged, because I could only get the gist of what the pastor was saying and felt lost. The singing was often my favorite part of the service (and it is in English, too) because it was repetitive and I could catch on quickly. Not being able to communicate with others clearly was extremely difficult for me as a verbal processor. But again, God gave me the skills I needed as I continued to practice, and I attended a bilingual church that was a huge blessing to me during my time in Chihuahua.

My second year in Mexico, I lived in a little house all by myself that was on the same property as La Casita Amarilla. In fact, it was La Casitita Amarilla, because it was even smaller. This little house was a bit like an in-law suite, with a small kitchen, bedroom, and bathroom — that's it. You could call it a tiny house, if you will (but it was bigger than a tiny house, because that's only cool on TV, not in real life). This little house was the first place that was all my own. What was so perfect about living in this house was that I was independent, but not completely alone. I had my own space, but living right behind me in my old house were my friends, mentors, and surrogate parents, Kevin and Wendy Case. They were so kind to me, and I was so grateful to have them around. Every now and then I would go to their house for dinner, or Wendy and I would walk in the park. I affectionately called them "Mama Wendy" and "Papa Kevin." I'll never forget when Wendy emailed my mom to get my favorite dessert recipe and made it for my birthday, or when they took me on my very first overnight camping trip! It was a perfect provision from the Lord for me to have older and wiser friends who were a stone's throw away whenever I needed them.

As an extrovert who loves to be around people and draws energy from others, it was difficult for me to acclimate to a quiet house that seemed so empty. But in time, I found that the Lord had given me the sweetest little gift in living alone. Living on your own can be an incredible experience when you choose to appreciate it and milk it for all its worth. I could sing praise and worship songs (and Adele, duh) as loud as I wanted to, and if I didn't feel like cleaning up after dinner, it didn't matter. No one was there to get annoyed! Living alone can be a huge blessing and a growth period if you let it. I loved my freedom and enjoyed learning more about myself and my preferences while also growing closer to Jesus.

It was in this little house where I would learn to cry out to the Lord and surrender and re-surrender my love life (or lack thereof) to Him. It was here where I truly began to understand what I believed, as I was completely on my own in a foreign place with not a familiar friend in sight. There were many valleys in which I came to know that Jesus would be the only constant in my life and my first love. It was becoming more and more clear to me that He would be the only thing in my life that literally would never change.

The Lord has given me the gift of being able to adapt in various situations — at least outwardly. I enjoy learning about other cultures and experiencing life in a way that is unlike my norm. The people of Mexico are incredible; their hospitality is unrivaled. I remember walking through my neighborhood and getting to know families there. One sweet lady and her granddaughter became dear friends to me. I would walk a few blocks to their house, and they invited me, a perfect stranger, into their home. One time, they came over to my house and learned how to make peanut butter cookies, and they returned the favor by allowing me to come watch how to make a special Mexican bread pudding at a family member's house. One Saturday morning, I was walking in my neighborhood and walked by my landlady's house. She saw me, welcomed me in, and we talked for over an hour! This type of hospitality and willingness to just connect with the people around you for the sake of connection was something I had not experienced in the United States, and I soaked it all in, hoping I could learn something from this exquisite culture. Living outside of my own comfort zone was an incredible experience, and I wanted to glean all I could from the incredible people the Lord placed in my path.

During my time in Mexico, I remember attending a women's retreat with my church that was so perfectly timed as a balm for my soul. At this retreat, we walked through the book of Ruth and learned about what it meant to be a sojourner who was captivated by the one true God. If you're not familiar with the narrative of Ruth, it is truly one of the most fascinating stories of the Bible. Ruth was the daughter-in-law of Naomi. When Ruth's husband died, she made the brave and humble decision to stay with her mother-in-law Naomi instead of abandoning her and moving on to live her own life. This decision was one of uncommon and sacrificial kindness. When a woman was widowed in Biblical times, it was an unofficial death sentence. A woman had no means of providing for herself and was unable to survive without the provision of a man. Ruth's decision to stay with Naomi was unheard of and unprecedented, yet God used it in incredible ways in not only her life, but the lives of so many around her.

The beautiful thing about Ruth's story is that she was bold and different. She didn't follow the status quo, but instead was a woman of humility, grace, and courage. When both Naomi and Ruth found themselves as widows, stuck and trying to figure out their next steps, Orpah, Naomi's other daughter-in-law, decided to get out of dodge. But Ruth made an extraordinary decision by choosing to stay with Naomi. Naomi's name means "sweet and pleasant" in Hebrew, but when she returns to Bethlehem after losing her husband and two sons, she says, "Do not call me Naomi; call me Mara, for the Almighty has dealt very bitterly with me" (Ruth 1:20). Mara means "bitter" in Hebrew. Naomi was in a pit of deep grief and in need of a true and loyal friend. Ruth's name means "friend" or "companion" in Hebrew. How apt are the names given to these women? Naomi, a once sweet and pleasant woman, is now defined by her bitterness. But Ruth, her daughter-in-law, refuses to leave her there. She commits to caring for her in her grief, which is the mark of a genuine friend. As a Moabitess, Ruth was not welcome in Naomi's land. Naomi was an Israelite, and her people group were chosen by God.

Ruth would not have known the customs and came from a land of people who worshipped pagan gods and did not know the one true God. But Ruth boldly says to Naomi: "Do not urge me to leave you or to return from following you. For where you go I will go, and where you lodge I will lodge. Your people shall be my people, and your God my God. Where you die I will die, and there will I be buried. May the Lord do so to me and more also if anything but death parts me from you" (Ruth 1:16-17).

Do you know what is even more amazing about Ruth's story? It is not about her. Yes, it is easy to read the book and be amazed at her honorable attributes. But my friend, the book of Ruth is about the greatness of God and His provision. The book of Ruth is "a picture of selflessness being a canvas God uses to paint His story of redemption. Grace is the brush, humility is the canvas, and God's faithfulness is the paint."1 It is about the kindness of a wise and loving Father who desires to give good gifts to His children. In the first chapter of Ruth, we find her hopeless and desolate as a foreigner in a strange land. Yet by the end of the book, we rejoice with her as she marries Boaz and gives birth to a son who not only would be in the lineage of King David, but King Jesus.

Only God can make something out of nothing. Through the entire book of Ruth, we see God's protection and provision for His beloved. When Ruth and Naomi show up on the scene in Bethlehem (which ironically means "house of bread" in Hebrew), they are hungry, penniless widows. And yet God in His wisdom had already begun to work in the background to give them exactly what they need. In Leviticus 19:10, He instructed the Israelites to allow the "poor and the sojourner" to glean from the edges of the field in order to ensure their survival. When Ruth gleaned from the fields for one day, she went home with more than an ephah of grain. This was equivalent to 22 liters and was a few weeks' worth of labor! But isn't this just like our God? He gives above and beyond what we can ask for because He "doesn't give us His grace in small portions and He never does things in 'halves.'"[1]

Ruth began to work in a field belonging to a man named Boaz, and because she was a woman of honorable repute, he took note of her. What is remarkable about this story is that Ruth began to work in the field of a man who "just so happened to be" her kinsman-redeemer. This was yet another striking example of God's provision for His people. A kinsman-redeemer was a relative who would pledge to marry and care for a widow, and she would be under his covering and protected from poverty and a life of shame. Boaz not only allowed Ruth to work in his fields, he protected her and provided for her, all before they were even a couple! These character traits portrayed a man of God who was reputable, honorable, and worthy of great respect. And Boaz is not the only one who deserves our respect here, friends. Ruth's boldness and courage were refreshing and altogether different, and after a strange proposal, (you've got to go read it, friend) God allowed them to marry and then begin a family of their own.

Here is what captivated my heart as I dove into the story of Ruth: God's kindness and everlasting love. Ruth may have felt forgotten and abandoned, but the exact opposite was true. God orchestrated the most beautifully redemptive love story for her in His timing and His way. And this story is not just about the romantic love we witness between Ruth and Boaz. Ruth goes from being a Moabite woman who worshipped pagan gods to one who declares that Yahweh, the one true God, is her God as well. This story is also a love story between a woman and her God. In the Bible, we see God's kindness woven through every single book. His love and faithfulness are evidence of His great kindness to us, and when we allow Him, He can open our eyes to see just how much He loves us. The Hebrew term for this kind of love is hesed. In *Steadfast Love*, Lauren Chandler writes:

> *Hesed is a term not so easily encapsulated in English. Various versions of the Bible and various appearances of the word in each version translate it into "faithfulness," "goodness," "kindness," "loyalty," "mercy," and "steadfast*

love." The simplest definition, however, is "loyal love." It is the committed, unchanging, loving determination of the Lord who will never give up on those whom He has chosen for Himself.[2]

When all I could do was focus on the fact that I was single, I could not see the beauty and the hesed love of God all around me. I defined myself by my singleness instead of by my security and identity in Christ. But God was always there, moving and working, sending reminders of His love for me and helping me to know Him more. When I was so laser-focused (read: obsessed!) with finding a mate, I could not see those things. I could not see that God was wooing and romancing me, helping me to develop a deeper relationship with Him as He revealed Himself to me. After yet another "pseudo-relationship" (This time with someone from the States! I have Facebook Messenger to thank for that one.), I knew that it was time to get serious. Was I going to continue my boy-crazy ways, or was Jesus going to be my everything?

During this season, I began to pray fervently and specifically for my future husband after reading a book called *Praying for Your Future Husband: Preparing Your Heart for His.*[3] My favorite Scripture to pray over him was Psalm 112 (as recommended by my sweet friend Gretchen), and I also began writing letters to him. I longed to meet him and see his face. I prayed like I had never prayed before and saturated myself in God's word. During this time, I began to pray earnestly asking the Lord to protect him, whoever he might be and wherever he was. I prayed for the Lord to guide him and lead him. I prayed the would know the goodness of God's love and that his heart would be prepared for mine.

You see, I had a rich and full life in Mexico, but I was surrounded by families. I constantly saw what I hoped my future would one day look like, and sometimes it was just painful. However, there was so much beauty in the midst of this pain. A missionary family unofficially adopted me, and I found so much fulfillment and affirmation in getting to be a part of life with them. The dad, Sean, was the pastor of my church, and his wife, Lisa, was my Bible study leader, mentor, and friend. Plus, I taught one of their four daughters, Quincy, in my class during both of my years at the school. Our lives intersected in the best of ways, and I saw them almost every day for those two years. They kindly and generously brought me in during holidays and other times when I would have otherwise been alone.

As a young single woman, this time with the Rafferty family was invaluable to me. I got to hang out with a family, see how they lived life, and also got an up-close look at a wonderfully godly marriage. They let me in, and I devoured the time that I had with them. We had movie nights, Thanksgiving dinners, birthday parties, and sleepovers, and it was all amazing. They are still some of my closest friends, and I've visited them in Colorado where they now live, and they have come to see me in Athens! I am hopefully expectant that we will be friends for life.

Friend, I tell you about my experiences with other families as a source of encouragement. If you are single, pray for and seek out a family that you can hang with. It may seem weird or awkward to you to do so, but there is so much joy in living day-to-day life with a family when you are used to being on your own. You are a part of something that everyone desires, whether they admit or not, and this sense of belonging is so wonderful. If you are married, be sure to include your single friends in your life. Getting married does not allow you entrance into a secret club. It is not an achievement or a rite of passage. When we allow others into our lives, regardless of their marital status, we all benefit.

The Lord provided for me in every season in every way, because that's what hesed does. That's who He is. But I wanted to find love in the worst way, and it just did not seem to want to find me. I began to search my heart and wondered if I was hoping in the Lord to fulfill my dreams and just give me what I wanted or if I was truly delighting in His presence. Was I content to walk through life side by side with Him, or did I want Him to just be the fulfiller of my dreams?

Chapter 5

The Power of Prayer

*Do not be anxious about anything, but in everything by prayer
and supplication with thanksgiving, let your requests be made
known to God. And the peace of God, which surpasses all
understanding, will guard your hearts and minds in Christ Jesus.
- Philippians 4:6-7*

We often underestimate the power of prayer, treating it as a last resort and not considering the power we unleash in the heavens when we come to God in earnest humility. Our attitudes toward prayer are often lazy and lackadaisical. But God considers prayer to be paramount to other courses of action. In reading the book Praying for Your Future Husband, I was challenged to create a list. In middle school, I remember thinking about the attributes and characteristics of a future husband that were most desirable to me. At this time, six pack abs, bulging biceps, and a tall stature were what rounded out my list. But this new list focused on the internal character of a man who loved God.

Not only was I challenged to make a list of characteristics for my future husband, but the author also stated the importance of praying for yourself — that God would mold and shape you into the person you know He has created you to be. So, while I still hoped for those chiseled abs, my desires shifted, and my prayers became much more intentional.

My desired character traits for a husband:

- A good listener
- Compassionate, generous
- Conforms to God, not to the world
- Dependable

- Has a sense of humor
- Humble
- Obedient
- Pure
- Sincere
- Trusts God's timing

Character traits I desire(d) to possess:

- Bold
- Content
- Diligent
- Faithful
- Has endurance
- Joyful and thankful
- Secure
- Seeks God's wisdom
- Thorough
- Works for the Lord, not for man

It's often said that the purpose of prayer is not to change God, it's to change us. When we take the time to gaze upon Him instead of being laser-focused on our circumstances, there is power. There is strength in humility and self-forgetfulness. There is beauty in gazing upon the might and majesty of a God who knows all and is in all. And while there is nothing magical about making a list, power resides in intentional and focused prayer. Let's consider a few examples in Scripture where God moved in response to the prayers of His people:

- Elijah prayed for rain and after three years of drought, it rained. (James 5:17)
- Anna prayed in the temple awaiting the promised Messiah and He came to earth. (Luke 2:36-38)
- Moses prayed and interceded on behalf of the Israelites in order to turn away God's wrath and God had mercy. (Exodus 32:7-14)
- Hezekiah prayed for healing and for God to spare his life and was given fifteen more years to live. (2 Kings 20:12-21)

There is beauty and power when we come before the Lord in surrender with open hands saying, "I can't do this. You have to take control." He honors that and sees us, and He wants us to know Him more as a result. How often do we say that we are trusting the Lord but act as though everything and everyone depends on us? How often do we worry and fret over things that are completely out of our hands and refuse to rest in His grace and mercy?

If we are going to walk through this life victoriously instead of feeling sorry for ourselves and pining away for a life we are not living, we have got to replace the lies with the truth. The only way to do this is to gird ourselves with the armor of God. This armor is central to a victorious Christian life. In Ephesians 6, Paul encourages the people of the church to get serious about how they walk out their faith:

Finally, be strong in the Lord and in the strength of his might. Put on the whole armor of God, that you may be able to stand against the schemes of the devil. For we do not wrestle against flesh and blood, but against the rulers, against the authorities, against the cosmic powers over this present darkness, against the spiritual forces of evil in the heavenly places. Therefore, take up the whole armor of God, that you may be able to withstand in the evil day, and having done all, to stand firm. Stand therefore, having fastened on the belt of truth, and having put on the breastplate of righteousness, and, as shoes for your feet, having put on the readiness given by the gospel of peace. In all circumstances take up the shield of faith, with which you can extinguish all the flaming darts of the evil one; and take the helmet of salvation, and the sword of the Spirit, which is the word of God, praying at all times in the Spirit, with all prayer and supplication. - Ephesians 6:10-18

Friend, we have a very real enemy of our souls. This enemy does not want to see us thrive and prosper. He does not want us to walk in wholeness and victory each day. He wants us feeling stuck, repeating negative patterns of behavior, and wallowing in self-pity. The subject of spiritual warfare may be one with which you are not familiar, and if not, that's another book entirely! So why do I mention it in a book about love and dating and marriage? Because it is real, and it affects every single aspect of our lives.

My decision to pray for my future husband was rooted in a sense of understanding and belief that my prayers were heard. I knew that even if the situations around me did not reflect the realization of my ultimate dreams and desires, God had surely not forgotten about me. The enemy of my soul wanted me to believe I was alone, abandoned, and forgotten. But the Bible assured me that I was seen, known, and loved by my Heavenly Father. You see, the tools we are given in the armor of God are all vital and necessary to be able to live a life full of hope, joy, and trust in our good Father. But the beautiful thing about these tools is that they are activated when we pray.1

Sometimes as I prayed, I felt as though my prayers were not getting anywhere. I also felt a little crazy. I mean, what if I was not ever going to get married? Why spend my time praying for someone I did not even know existed? God continued to assure me that time with Him was never time wasted, and He led me to various examples in Scripture where other women also felt unseen or unheard.

In 1 Samuel 2, we see a stunning example of a woman who prayed diligently and discovered just how much her God loved her as she watched Him move in her life. Hannah was a woman with a desire for a child, but she found herself disappointed as weeks, months, and years went by with no child to speak of. In Biblical times, children were a mark of honor and distinction, and sons were needed in order to work the land and carry on the family line. Men often had more than one wife, and Hannah's "sister-wife," Peninnah was the complete opposite of Hannah. While Hannah was barren, Peninnah had several children. Each year, when they went to worship and offer sacrifices to God as a family, Peninnah taunted Hannah in the midst of her pain. During this painful time, Hannah's husband, Elkanah, gave her a double portion in hopes that her heart would be encouraged. He said to her, "Am I not more to you than ten sons?" (1 Samuel 1:8)

But Hannah could not deny the desire deep within her heart. Everything within her longed for a child, and the love of her husband, while sweet and kind, was not enough to satisfy that desire. In the midst of her sorrow and desperation, Hannah sought God through weeping on her knees at the temple. Her prayer is one of the most vulnerable and gut-wrenching prayers we see in Scripture. Let's take a look at her story.

After they had eaten and drunk in Shiloh, Hannah rose. Now Eli the priest was sitting on the seat beside the doorpost of the temple of the Lord. She was deeply distressed and prayed to the Lord and wept bitterly. And she vowed a vow and said, "O Lord of hosts, if you will indeed look on the affliction of your servant and remember me and not forget your servant, but will give to your servant a son, then I will give him to the Lord all the days of his life, and no razor shall touch his head."

As she continued praying before the Lord, Eli observed her mouth. Hannah was speaking in her heart; only her lips moved, and her voice was not heard. Therefore, Eli took her to be a drunken woman. And Eli said to her, "How long will you go on being drunk? Put your wine away from you." But Hannah answered, "No, my lord, I am a woman troubled in spirit. I have drunk neither wine nor strong drink, but I have been pouring out my soul before the Lord. Do not regard your servant as a worthless woman, for all along I have been speaking out of my great anxiety and vexation." Then Eli answered, "Go in peace, and the God of Israel grant your petition that you have made to him." And she said, "Let your servant find favor in your eyes." Then the woman went her way and ate, and her face was no longer sad.

They rose early in the morning and worshiped before the Lord; then they went back to their house at Ramah. And Elkanah knew Hannah his wife, and the Lord remembered her. And in due time Hannah conceived and bore a son, and she called his name Samuel, for she said, "I have asked for him from the Lord." - 1 Samuel 1:9-20

Friend, there is so much to learn from this beautiful story. We know Hannah was a woman who had been barren for years. She was a sister-wife to a woman who was mean and unfeeling, and yet we do not read of any retaliation or bitterness toward this woman (although we could argue that it seems like she would deserve it!). Her desire to be a mother was genuine, yet difficult to bear. Hannah found herself in a period of waiting that seemed like it would never end. Can you relate?

When Eli, the priest, saw Hannah, he thought she was drunk! She was muttering words and begging God for His favor and blessing, and she denied his accusation by explaining her situation. Romans 8:26 tells us that

> *the Holy Spirit helps us in our weakness. For we do not know what to pray for as we ought, but the Spirit Himself intercedes for us with groaning too deep for words. And he who searches hearts knows what is the mind of the Spirit, because the Spirit intercedes for the saints according to the will of God.*

When you are distraught and find yourself with no words, the Holy Spirit has not left you. He is right there with you, interceding on your behalf and going to God the Father in order to bring about the good in your life that you so desire. It just may look a little different than you were imagining. Friend, when was the last time you were completely honest with God about your situation? Sometimes, in the name of being "brave" or "grateful," we plaster on a smile and tell everyone that we are fine. But it is ok to not be ok. One of the sweetest parts of being in relationship with God is the vulnerability we can have when we come to Him. He sees us, He knows us, and He loves us.

I remember attending an out of town wedding where I would not know many people, and of course, I was dateless. It was one of the more difficult experiences of my singleness, and I confess I was miserable. I cried in the hotel room and struggled to find joy in the midst of a social situation where I was so obviously unattached and alone. I watched other couples and was so very lonely and jealous because romantic love seemed like a reality that would never be a part of my life. My heart physically ached, and I yearned for an ending to this not-so-pleasant chapter of my story. I did not understand why it hurt so much and why I had not been able to find much relief, and I was emotionally exhausted from trying to come up with some kind of solution. I just wanted to fix it, and my idea of fixing it was to find a mate.

During this time, I was beginning to wonder if there was something wrong with me. I imagine Hannah may have felt the same way, don't you? Year after year, she prayed and asked the Lord to open her womb. But year after year, God said no (or so it seemed). In this instance, God said, "Not yet." Even without knowing what was to come, she still kept hoping against hope. In Hannah's beautiful prayer following her miracle, she exalts God and gives Him all of the glory for giving her a son and answering her prayer. She does not gloat and poke at Peninnah or say, "I told you so!" She does not become a helicopter mom and keep Samuel to herself. She gives him right back to God, knowing that this great blessing would not have been possible if not for His lovingkindness.

"Our soul waits for the Lord; He is our help and our shield. For our heart is glad in Him, because we trust in His holy name. Let your steadfast love, O Lord, be upon us, even as we hope in you." - Psalm 33:20-22

"I sought the Lord, and He answered me and delivered me from all my fears. Those who look to Him are radiant, and their faces shall never be ashamed... The Lord is near to the brokenhearted and saves the crushed in spirit."
- Psalm 34:4-5, 18

The Psalms have always been a balm to my soul, because their words are perfect for every season. When I read verses like the ones above, I am reminded of the perfect goodness of my loving Heavenly Father. When I wait for Him instead of waiting on whatever change in my circumstances that I think will bring me peace and joy, my heart is "glad in Him." When I seek Him, I find that His ways are higher and His peace passes all understanding. When I look to Him instead of keeping my head down in the midst of my sometimes-disappointing circumstances, I am radiant, and I will never. be. ashamed.

Shame can tell us all kinds of lies that will have us believing we are fools for hoping. But throughout God's word, we are told to hope. Not to hope in the perfect Pinterest life, but to hope in an unfailing, never changing, always with us God. The word "hope" is mentioned in the Bible over 100 times. I think this means God knew we would need to speak to our souls in order to remind them of the importance of remembering His faithfulness.

Maybe you're waiting for God to bring you a mate. Maybe you're waiting for God to bring you a baby or to reconcile a relationship that is not in a healthy place. Maybe you're waiting to hear back about the test results from the doctor. Maybe you're waiting to get a letter of acceptance or rejection from a school or a new job. Whatever you're waiting for, we all know waiting can seem like the worst lot of all when there is something we desire that has not yet come to fruition. The waiting season can feel volatile and unpredictable. As humans, we enjoy a sense of control over our lives. When we are waiting on something, we are faced with the reality that there is truly very little in our lives we can actually control.

We like to take credit for the "achievements" in our lives, don't we? I chose the college I attended. I chose my major. I chose my first job. I chose my car. I chose my friends. None of those seem like false statements, but when we think about them and evaluate them in light of eternity, we may realize that we can take little to no credit for the trajectory of our lives. God, in His sovereign grace and mercy, orchestrates our lives. Yes, we have free will, but He brings us to certain people and places for His specific purpose. It is God who uses these things in our lives in order to shape us and make us more like Him, if we let Him do so.

When we think about prayer, we often think we need to be able to say the right words in order to receive the desired result. But prayer is not a manipulative tool that we use to change God. It is a two-way conversation. When we pray, He strengthens our heart while He reveals to us His true character. Prayer is not a shortcut to getting what you want or fixing your life. Prayer is our very lifeline. Martin Luther wisely stated, "To be a Christian without praying is no more possible than to be alive without breathing," and "I have so much to do that I shall spend the first three hours in prayer." Do we think about prayer as our very lifeline? Do we consider it to be as important as our next breath and worthy of the first moments of our every day?

How often do we choose other steps to take instead of prayer? It is so much easier to text or call a friend, complain to a coworker, sleep in a little later, or watch another episode on Netflix instead of intentionally communing with our Heavenly Father. But friend, when we prioritize prayer and allow God to reveal Himself to us, He promises to tell us things! Jeremiah 33:3 says, "Call to me, and I will answer you and tell you great and hidden things that you have not known." That sounds like a deal I want to get in on! I want to know God more through prayer, not just come to Him with my list of wishes and to-dos. When we come to God, asking for Him to fulfill our desires and answer our prayers, we must examine our hearts. Why do we want what we are asking for?

I confess to you that as I waited and waited and waited some more, oftentimes my heart was not in the right place. My prayers were often selfish, as I had a specific answer in mind - the end to my singleness. Yes, my desire for a spouse was real, but I also believed many things that were not true about what would happen when God "finally" brought me that person. I wanted to be "equal" or "as good as" my friends who were already married. I wanted to not be lonely anymore. And let's be honest, I wanted a diamond ring. But God did not choose to immediately answer in that way. Instead, He chose to help me understand how to live my life with my hands open, trusting that whatever His plan was, it would be so much better than mine. As I continued to pour out my heart before Him, journaling was often my preferred means of communication. I filled page after page with my feelings, thoughts, hopes, dreams and expectations. In turn, He responded by giving me passages of Scripture that seemed to jump off the page, song lyrics that seemed to be written just for me, and words of encouragement from friends that were so perfectly timed, it was eerie. Through praying for my future husband, God taught me that prayer is not about me. We can use prayer to move heaven and earth, but sometimes, He moves heaven and earth within us and leads us to a deeper place of knowing and trusting Him that we would not have otherwise experienced.

Chapter 6

Recognizing the Lies

"Define yourself as one radically loved by God. This is your true self; every other identity is an illusion." - Brennan Manning

Friend, let's be honest. Sometimes being single sucks. But here's the truth. Singleness is not a curse. Singleness isn't something to get rid of or to treat like it's a disease. It's a gift. It doesn't always feel like it, but it is. How do I know that? Because anything the Lord gives us is a gift. An episode of a podcast called The Happy Hour with Jamie Ivey[1] gave me a completely different perspective on how I view God and my desires. In this podcast, Jamie interviews women who are walking with Christ in many different ways, callings, and seasons. Her guest for this episode, Tara Leigh Cobble was incredible, and she spoke so much truth that has stuck with me and been rattling around in my head ever since.

She spoke of how when we have a misconception of who God is, we are not living the way He wants us to nor allowing His character to influence how we respond to what He chooses to give us. There are many single people, she says, who are angry with God because He has not yet given them a spouse. I was one of them for a while. But God, she says, is always kind. If what God does is always kind, then whatever situation He has put us in is His ultimate kindness to us.

Y'all. This was mind-blowing to me. I only wish I had grasped this when I was single. Heck, I wish I could grasp it now. We always want what we do not yet have. And yet God. is. kind. Always. Everything He does is an extension of His love for us. We have to keep our wits about us when we are tempted to despair and believe that He has forgotten about us. The opposite of that thought is this truth: He could never forget about us, and He never will. We are His beloved. Even when we are in the midst of a desert season or still in the waiting, "His thoughts for us outnumber the grains of sand." (Psalm 139:17-18) This God of ours is not someone who is withholding from us or delighting in our misery.

So, can we bring Him our questions, our fears, and our longings? The answer is a resounding yes. But we can also hope and pray that in whatever season we find ourselves, may He be most glorified and our lives and thoughts be consumed with Him and His goodness. Our world is fleeting, friend. Marriage itself is for life here on earth, but heaven is waiting, and we must place our hopes there, where our Christ will forever be all we want and need. Deuteronomy 6:4-9 states,

> *Hear, O Israel: The Lord our God, the Lord is one. You shall love the Lord your God with all your heart and with all your soul and with all your might. And these words that I command you today shall be on your heart. You shall teach them diligently to your children, and shall talk of them when you sit in your house, and when you walk by the way, and when you lie down, and when you rise. You shall bind them as a sign on your hand, and they shall be as frontlets between your eyes. You shall write them on the doorposts of your house and on your gates.*

It's your choice. Who are you going to listen to? God says His word is eternal, unchanging, and life-giving. Are you pouring the word of God into your heart, mind, and soul? Or are you listening to the advice of well-meaning friends and the voices of pop culture? You've got to make a choice. Will you believe what He says and choose to live like it is true?

In Genesis 16, we encounter a story in which two women are desperate for the lovingkindness of a merciful God. Abram's wife Sarai was having trouble conceiving a child. You may know that God promises this couple a family so big that the descendants outnumber the stars. Well friend, this promise does not come until Genesis 17. Genesis 16 shows us what can happen when we tire of waiting on God and decide to take matters into our own hands. Sarai was older and had long thought she would never conceive.

Most likely all of her friends had already been able to do so, and at this point, they probably had great-grandchildren. But poor Sarah was left barren year after year, decade after decade with no child of her own. She watched other people live the dream that remained unfulfilled for her, and I can imagine she was often tempted with bitterness, anger, and jealousy. We can all exhibit those kinds of behaviors when we left wanting, can't we?

When Sarai was just completely done with waiting, she decided to go to her maidservant, Hagar, and ask if she would bear a child on her behalf. Think of it like a surrogate pregnancy but without the, ahem, technology. This practice, while not godly, was common in Biblical times because the family line was of utmost importance. After Sarai mentioned this to her husband, Abram, he said that he was willing to do whatever needed to be done. When Sarai found out that Hagar was pregnant, an inevitable jealousy grew within her, and their already fragile relationship was further poisoned. Hagar began to feel as though she had a leg up on Sarai, and when Sarai had enough of that attitude, Hagar ran away! Can you imagine? Hagar had no "good name" to speak of and was a poor servant girl who had been taken advantage of by her master and mistress. When this treatment was too much, she retaliated and then found she could no longer endure a home environment where she was not welcome. When we come to the end of Genesis 16, we find Hagar in a completely vulnerable situation. Let's take a closer look at her story.

> The angel of the Lord found her by a spring of water in the wilderness, the spring on the way to Shur. And he said, "Hagar, servant of Sarai, where have you come from and where are you going?" She said, "I am fleeing from my mistress Sarai." The angel of the Lord said to her, "Return to your mistress and submit to her." The angel of the Lord also said to her, "I will surely multiply your offspring so that they cannot be numbered for multitude." And the angel of the Lord said to her, "Behold, you are pregnant and shall bear a son. You shall call his name Ishmael, because the Lord has listened to your affliction. He shall be a wild donkey of a man, his hand against everyone and everyone's hand against him, and he shall dwell over against all his kinsmen."

So she called the name of the Lord who spoke to her, "You are a God of seeing," for she said, "Truly here I have seen him who looks after me." Therefore the well was called Beer-lahai-roi; it lies between Kadesh and Bered.

And Hagar bore Abram a son, and Abram called the name of his son, whom Hagar bore, Ishmael. Abram was eighty-six years old when Hagar bore Ishmael to Abram.

This story offers us many lessons. First, we see that Sarai was not willing to wait on God's timing and His perfect plan for her life. She believed that she was not enough because she was not yet a mama. When she took matters into her own hands, she decided to "outsmart" God and rush the process because she was unable to see any other way. And Abram? Goodness, did he ever need to man up! Yes, God redeemed their story and there is grace that covers a multitude of sin, but wow is it painful to see Abram's apathy in this situation. And last but not least, we come to Hagar. Poor, sweet Hagar. Most likely, Hagar did not have a very enjoyable life. She was likely ignored and snubbed by many people. Yet Hagar seemed determined to hope. When the script was flipped, she snubbed Sarai, but she so desperately wanted to hold on to hope after being cast out.

Have you ever been tempted to take matters into your own hands when the waiting seemed unbearable? Maybe you've forced or manipulated situations to make them go your way. Maybe you've sown seeds in all the wrong places in order to get attention from a potential suitor who really wasn't God's best for you. Maybe you've questioned God's goodness because life just seemed too hard and complicated.

In the midst of Hagar and Sarai's awfully dramatic relationship, God was there. When all hope seemed lost and the plan blew up in everyone's faces, God was there. When Sarai's manipulation proved unsuccessful and when Hagar doubted her worth, God was there. Sarai saw Hagar as an inconvenience and as competition, but God saw Hagar as beloved. He knew everything that was going on in her mind, and He loved her too much to leave her in the midst of the heartache. The angel of the Lord not only spoke directly to Hagar, he gave her the courage she needed to go back and face the woman who had cast her out. I can only imagine what God taught Hagar through her sorrow and how He used her boldness and courage to encourage Sarai to look to Him for her provision. A common thread is woven through this story as we watch the characters make decisions rooted not in truth, but rather in lies. When we do the same, we jeopardize God's peace in our lives and invite the enemy of our souls to wreak havoc within and around us.

On August 27, 2014, just a couple months before I met my future husband, I wrote the following in my journal:

Lord, I am so tired of being single. I am so tired of being so mentally preoccupied with how not to be single. I am so tired of comparing my life to others'. I am so tired of feeling less than. I am so tired of being so emotional and so seemingly immature about boys and relationships due to my lack of experience. I am mostly very tired of waiting. I am so prone to the lies of the enemy, because he has gotten craftier and craftier by not being so forward, but rather sneaking into thought patterns and processes. Damn him. Hate that guy.

One of my students, Kevin, was so open with me today. He said to me, "I think Satan is in my mind." And I told him to fight that voice with Scripture. I really need to take my own advice. Lord, help me to feast upon Your word. Help me to know it well and walk in freedom, because the truth sets people free. I want to be free. I want to be brave. I want to be fearless. Help me, Lord.

I am convinced that the root of all our problems in this life is in deception. It goes back to the Garden — the serpent deceived Eve, and he has persisted ever since. There are 10 common lies that we are tempted to believe when we're waiting on God to fulfill His promises to us, and I think it is time we unpack each one of those lies and begin to walk in the truth.

Chapter 7

Getting Rid of the Lies

"Take your cue about you from the one who made you, loves you, redeemed you...and the one who calls you his masterpiece."
- Sandra Stanley

One of the most difficult parts of walking with Christ is rehearsing truth and preaching the Gospel to yourself every. single. day. It is easy to take the truth for granted or to get comfortable and to forget what God has done for you and what it means for your life. But God's mercies are new every morning, and because He is always good, we can know, believe, and receive His truth and then walk in it! Let's take a look at some common lies that we believe when we are in a seemingly unending era of waiting.

Lie 1: You are less than because you are single.
Truth: You are made whole with a purpose.
God's Word: For we are His workmanship, created in Christ Jesus for good works; which God has prepared beforehand, that we should walk in them. - Ephesians 2:10

It is incredibly easy to get caught in the comparison trap, isn't it? When we look at others' lives around us and feel like they are somehow doing better or have arrived, discouragement is quick to settle in. During my singleness, I often felt like I was left behind when so many friends were running down the aisle. I also felt like my time was not seen as valuable because I did not have a husband or kids. This school of thought seemed unfair to me. No, I was not attached to anyone, but that didn't mean that I was just twiddling my thumbs as I waited for Prince Charming to come. I had a full life and enjoyed my friends. I did not want to be called upon to volunteer for every activity just because I was "single with nothing to do."

Here's the thing about singleness that I think the church (and we) are not exactly doing right — we do not know what to do with single people. There are Sunday school classes, small groups, and events that are completely planned around married folks with or without kids. But there are not many options for the YoPros (young professionals — I sure do love my abbreviations). And us married people? We just want to marry off the singles because we love marriage so much! But friend, there is a better way.

While working on this book, I have had conversations with others about what they hope the church would do differently and how we could better treat the singles in our congregations. Here are some of the comments from friends:

I wish the church would do a better job of accepting that singleness is not any less than marriage — and teaching that to young people. So often I still encounter the idea that the only way anyone can be successful or fulfilled or happy is to be married. I also wish the church would do a better job incorporating singles into the body — not making everything a single or married thing. Plus, singles events and classes are often really awkward and feel too much like speed dating. Especially as you get older (and though I realize I'm not old, I am on the older end of singles for much of the south.)
- Brooke

I wish the church did a better job of not highlighting the singleness of young single people. We need community that is not "based" on a bunch of single people who (it seems like) "graduate" to married and family life classes/groups. Single folks need friendship and support as humans with needs, not as a further reminder that "you're on your own, kid."
- Natalie

One of the most important things to remember is that your life is valuable no matter what. If there is still breath in your lungs, God has a purpose for you. Do not put off what God has told you to do or push away dreams that you could go after right now just because you are waiting on a spouse. Your life can be a grand

46

adventure regardless of your marital status when you are walking with God!

Lie 2: Marriage is a reward and something you can earn.
Truth: All gifts come from God, and a gift cannot be earned.
God's Word: Do not be deceived, my beloved brothers. Every good and every perfect gift is from above, coming down from the Father of lights with whom there is no variation or shadow due to change. - James 1:16-17

When we begin to think of God as our Santa Claus, we are looking to Him to fulfill our wishes instead of be our everything. When we ask Him for things and He delays in bringing them to us, we have a choice. Will we believe that He is good, or will we try to take matters into our own hands like Sarai, Abram, and Hagar?

Believing God will fulfill our desires if we were "good enough" is flawed theology. It is easy to think we can perform and jump through hoops to get what we want, but the truth is that it is God alone who orchestrates our circumstances in order to bring about His perfect plan for our lives. People who are married have not "arrived." Everyone is in process, and God has His way of bringing about sanctification in each of our lives. For some it is through marriage, and for others, it is through singleness. Either way, God will get the glory when we delight in Him and trust Him to do the work of changing our hearts.

When we look at married people as better than our single counterparts, we miss out on learning from our brothers and sisters who have wisdom to offer that transcends marital status. My friend Tori said, "I think the church often looks to married women for advice, as if they have more insight or maturity simply because they are married." We have to understand that each person who is part of the body of Christ brings something unique and worthwhile to the table. Because God has ransomed us and made us new, we each have gifts we can use to further the Kingdom, married or not. God's gifts are not determined by our behavior. He is faithful and good, regardless of whether all of our dreams come true.

Lie 3: He will not be faithful to His word.
Truth: He is always faithful. Always.

ALREADY CHOSEN

God's Word: He who calls you is faithful; He will surely do it.
- 1 Thessalonians 5:24

Who are we to question God's character? We can take a look back at our lives and see how He has provided time after time after time. When we measure the truth of His goodness against our present circumstances, His love will always win. He gives and gives and gives, and His faithfulness never changes, because He never changes. He cannot deny Himself (2 Timothy 2:13). Consider these verses and then apply them to your life right now. Receive His truth and ask for a revelation from the Holy Spirit that is personal to you.

Know therefore that the Lord your God is God, the faithful God who keeps covenant and steadfast love with those who love him and keep his commandments, to a thousand generations. -Deuteronomy 7:9

All the paths of the Lord are steadfast love and faithfulness, for those who keep his covenant and his testimonies. - Psalm 25:10

For the word of the Lord is upright, and all his work is done in faithfulness. - Psalm 33:4

For the Lord God is a sun and shield; the Lord bestows favor and honor. No good thing does he withhold from those who walk uprightly. - Psalm 84:11

The steadfast love of the Lord never ceases; his mercies never come to an end; they are new every morning; great is your faithfulness. "The Lord is my portion," says my soul, "therefore I will hope in him."- Lamentations 3:22-24

O Lord, you are my God; I will exalt you; I will praise your name, for you have done wonderful things, plans formed of old, faithful and sure. - Isaiah 25:1

For all the promises of God find their Yes in him. That is why it is through him that we utter our Amen to God for his glory. - 2 Corinthians 1:20

Lie 4: You're the only one who knows how you feel.
Truth: He knows your every thought, and you are never alone.
God's Word: O Lord, you have searched me and known me!
You know when I sit down and when I rise up; you discern my
thoughts from afar. -Psalm 139:1

God created you with a purpose, on purpose. No
experience that you walk through is completely unique to you,
because there is nothing new under the sun. However, the enemy
of your soul knows if he can get you to believe you are alone, then
you are ineffective in your purpose here on earth. God's word tells
us we are comforted so that we can comfort others (2 Corinthians
1:3-5). He also says that He will never leave or forsake us
(Hebrews 13:5). He is by our side and will not abandon us to our
fears (Deuteronomy 31:8). He is our strong refuge (Psalm 46:1).
His word also says to cast all your anxiety on Him, because He
cares for you (1 Peter 5:7). When we fix our eyes on our troubles,
disappointments, and earthly things, the temptation to live from a
place of defeat can often overcome us. We see ourselves as victims
instead of conquerors. But friend, this is not the life God has for
us! He has a life for us that is full and abundant. The path to that
abundant life is found when we are honest with others about our
struggles, fears, and experiences. When we find community,
whether it is in a small group or with a prayer partner, we find
there are others with similar experiences who can help walk
alongside us. If you think you are the only one experiencing what
you are right now, ask God to provide a friend for you whom you
can confide in, and watch Him work through your transparency.

Lie 5: You are without hope.
Truth: Your hope is in Christ.
God's Word: We have this as a sure and steadfast anchor of
the soul, a hope that enters into the inner place behind the curtain.
-Hebrews 6:19

Is your hope in finding your perfect mate, or is your hope
in Christ alone? It is incredibly easy to place our hope in a change
of circumstances. But God does not call us to hope for a better
version of the life we are in now. He calls us to hope for a life
rooted in Him and consumed by Himself. In Ephesians, Paul prays
for the believers, asking "that the God of our Lord Jesus Christ, the
Father of glory, may give you the Spirit of wisdom and of

revelation in the knowledge of him, having the eyes of your hearts enlightened, that you may know what is the hope to which he has called you (Ephesians 1:17-18, emphasis mine). Friend, we are called to hope. When we fix our eyes on Jesus, He transforms our hearts and helps us to see as He sees. We realize what we have in Him, and everything we do not have begins to pale in comparison as we root and anchor our lives in His unfailing love and truth.

Lie 6: Your life will get better with marriage.
Truth: There are trials in all seasons.
God's Word: In this world, you will have tribulation. But take heart, I have overcome the world. - John 16:33

This lie may be the biggest one of all, friends. When we are constantly trying to get to the next stage, we believe the one we are in is not good enough. We essentially say to God, "This is not what I wanted, and I want to move on to what I think will satisfy me." If our attitude is one of discontent and ingratitude, we will never find true peace. I have heard it said that in marriage, the joy is doubled and the trials are halved. There is truth to this statement. There is nothing like knowing that you have someone to walk alongside in this crazy thing called life. But this person is not God, and they never will be. The truth is that living daily life face-to-face with another person can be extremely difficult, because you constantly stare your sin in the face. Who wants to sign up for that?! There are trials in every season of life, friends. Marriage does not absolve this reality, in fact, oftentimes the trials are more complicated! The truth we can cling to is that Christ equips us for all things, married or not.

Lie 7: Jesus is not enough.
Truth: Jesus is more than enough.
God's Word: The thief comes only to steal and kill and destroy. I came that they may have life and have it abundantly. - John 10:10

Ok, so I know I said the previous lie was the biggest one of all, but it actually may be this one that is the worst offender. When we believe "life will be better when x, y, z happens," we set ourselves up for disappointment. An abundant life finds its roots in truth and grace, which can only be found in Jesus. Abundant life is not Jesus plus the desires of our heart. Abundant life is

Jesus plus nothing else. Jesus plus nothing is our everything.2 The sooner we walk in this truth, the sooner we will know His peace.

Lie 8: It is ok to settle.
Truth: Never settle. God wants the best for you.
God's Word: Now to Him who is able to do far more abundantly than all that we ask or think, according to the power at work within us, to Him be glory in the church and in Christ Jesus throughout all generations.
- Ephesians 3:20-21

We have already stated that Jesus wants us to have an abundant life. Well friend, that abundant life will not be found when we settle for less than what He desires for us. Settling can take on many forms. We can decide to pursue a relationship with someone who we know is not good for us. We can put off and delay life goals in the fear that a relationship might come along. Whatever your version of settling is, remember God's desires for you are so much more. If He were to tell you of them, they would blow your mind. Trying to figure Him out or finding a way to make things happen on your own will not make you any happier. However, trusting what God says is true and resting in Him will change everything for you as you learn to walk with Him step by step, day by day.

Lie 9: Satisfy your desires with lust.
Truth: Value genuine love more than the fleeting passions of lust.
God's Word: Put to death, therefore what is earthly in you: sexual immorality, impurity, passion, evil desire, and covetousness, which is idolatry. - Colossians 3:5

It is quite easy for us to believe that lust is a problem that only men struggle with, but this is so far from the truth. Lust is such an easy trap to fall into because it is a classic "slippery slope" sin. Lust lies to us and tells us it is ok to get lost in our minds and entertain thoughts that we have no business entertaining. Lust is not limited to men or teenage boys, no, my friend, lust is something that women struggle with, too. And friend, there is no shame in that. There is no shame in lies and thoughts that enter your mind. The question is, what are you going to do with those thoughts? Will you allow yourself to continue down the path presented before you, or will you take your thoughts captive and make them obedient to Christ? (2 Corinthians 10:5)

One of my friends, Amy, wisely stated:

When it comes to sex, teach teens and young adults that it is a sacred, beautiful, wonderful part of a Godly marriage. It is not something scary or dirty to be feared, but something beautiful and special to be cherished. Also, while many churches are getting better about this, do not place the burden of sexual purity on women alone by telling them not to dress or act in ways that "tempt" young men into sin. Make sure men understand their responsibility in treating women with respect and setting their own boundaries against temptation. I grew up thinking lust and sexual desire were masculine traits and was thus surprised when I found myself faced with these temptations. Spend less time teaching girls how to not inspire lust in men and more time teaching them to understand and manage their own natural sexual desires.

We cannot continue to create a culture in which lust or sexual sin is the ultimate travesty and the unforgivable sin. Let's be honest with one another and hold each other accountable to seeking purity in every aspect of our lives. Lust is not just the scandalous thoughts that cross our minds, but the desires that remain unchecked. If we remember that surrender is a daily act, we will have the strength we need to fight the thoughts that oppose God's ways and will learn to continually walk in His might.

Lie 10: It is ok to feel sorry for yourself and be jealous of your friends.
Truth: There is power in contentment and gratitude for your current season.
God's Truth: Rejoice always, pray continually, give thanks in all circumstances.
- 1 Thessalonians 5:16-18

Every party has a pooper, doesn't it? But does your party have to have a pooper? Be honest with yourself. The life the Lord has given you is the only one you are going to have. And while it is so very tempting and easy to dwell on all you do not have, God never intended for us to wallow in self-pity. In fact, self-pity is the exact opposite of what He intends for us. The latter part of 1 Thessalonians 5:18 says, "give thanks in all circumstances, for this is the will of God in Christ Jesus for you" (emphasis mine). How often do we complain about not knowing God's will for our lives? How many times have we felt like we were floundering around and in the midst of a desperate time with no direction? As clear as day, God presents His will for us in His word: give thanks. We do not have to give thanks for all things, but in all things, we can thank Him.

When our eyes are fixed on all that we want and do not yet have, and we look around to the right and left and feel passed over and neglected, we can still find something good. Always. So what now, you ask? Speak truth over your circumstances, life, and feelings, and know that the Author of your soul loves you with a fierce and unrelenting love. Your life is good right now!

Chapter 8

Taking Chances

I've got this friend
Holding onto her heart
Like it's a little secret
Like it's all she's got to give
- The Civil Wars

After being a bridesmaid many times and continuing to pray through my singleness, I took a step back and realized I had some false beliefs. I said that I believed in my omnipotent God to provide, but I was unwilling to do much or take many risks that would allow Him to show up in an unexpected way. I had a thought in the back of my mind that said I should try online dating, because by this point I had a few friends who had successful experiences with it. But I just wasn't ready. However, in the spring of 2014, I read a book entitled *How to Get a Date Worth Keeping: Be Dating in Six Months or Your Money Back*.[1] I stumbled upon it one night on Amazon and was admittedly embarrassed to buy it. I mean, the title was soooo cheesy. But the authors were the same men who wrote the Boundaries books, so I figured I would give it a fair shot.

Well friend, this book kicked my butt. It made me realize how inactive I had been in my waiting on the Lord. Waiting on the Lord is not a passive activity, but rather an active pursuit of Him. In every other arena of my life, I took intentional steps to grab a hold of the things I wanted. When I thought about pursuing a post graduate degree, I took the GRE. When I wanted a new job, I went above and beyond to express interest and form a relationship with my potential employer. This tenacity served me well in these situations. So why wasn't I going for what I wanted in my dating life?

It was clear to me that I had decided to trust God in all areas of my life except for dating. Or maybe it was that I trusted Him too much! I expected Him to do all of the work and for a guy to just show up. I was too afraid to take leaps of faith in this area and didn't want to fall flat on my face. Because I had experienced rejection in various ways throughout my teen years, I wasn't ready to just "put myself out there." Have you ever seen the movie Never Been Kissed? A newspaper reporter in her late twenties goes back to high school and ends up falling in love with her teacher. I felt like this was my story (minus the sketchiness of falling in love with a teacher). I was definitely an anomaly as a kiss-less, boyfriend-less (as in, never had a boyfriend) girl in my late twenties. I thought I was making myself available, but I really wasn't. During this time, I was extremely busy and often overcommitted. I wore this busyness as a badge of honor, grateful that even though I did not have a significant other, at least I had a full life! But this busyness was constituted by hanging out with the same friends doing the same things. There weren't really opportunities in my life for me to meet new people because I hadn't created them. Yes, my life was full, and I enjoyed my new friendships and loved my church. But I wasn't taking any chances toward receiving the deepest desire of my heart.

One important tenet of *How to Get a Date Worth Keeping* is the importance of meeting new people. When you meet new people, you increase your chances of finding that person you're looking for. In order to meet new people, you've got to take some intentional steps. Do you like to run? Join a running club! Do you like coffee? Go to different coffee shops! And don't be afraid to ask your friends to set you up with their friends! You get the picture. In this book, the authors also addressed the stigma of online dating. Now friend, I am all about technology. I love social media and I have a blog, so obviously I am not anti-21st century. However, I had a big stigma with regards to online dating. I seriously thought it was for "those people." And when I say "those people," I mean people who were desperate. People who had no other options. Weirdos. Socially awkward folks. But when I read through that section of the book, I was seriously convicted! It seems silly, but I had to repent of my judgmental attitude and admit I was now one of "those people," because I was desperate!

ALREADY CHOSEN

In May 2014, I celebrated my 26th birthday. I had a running joke with some of my friends that if I did not marry by 25, I would join eHarmony. Well, year 25 came and went with no real prospects. I went on a couple dates, but nothing ever came of those, and it just wasn't quite right. So in June, I decided to put on my big girl panties and create a profile on eHarmony. I anxiously waited to see what would happen. Friends who have not tried online dating (which may be a small number of you with how popular it is now) please know — online dating is an interesting world. I had little to no experience when I signed up for eHarmony, and I was basically hoping that my $99 would be well invested. It was easy to get sucked into that world — I found myself checking my messages constantly and looking to see who viewed my profile. Within in a couple weeks, I ended up deleting the app from my phone in order to keep myself from going insane.

The summer of 2014 proved to be not at all what I expected. I traveled through most of the summer on mission trips and vacations. I had the privilege of traveling to Uganda on a mission trip with my church in May, which was incredible. For months and years prior, Uganda was on my heart. I didn't quite know why, but God kept placing stories from this country in my path, and I wanted to go and see it for myself. While in Uganda, I had the privilege of meeting some amazing men and women. We visited with and encouraged several different village churches and beheld faces full of the joy of the Lord. And it was good. So good. The journey to Uganda was so clearly marked by the Lord, and even though I knew I was supposed to go, I wasn't sure why I went.

On one of our last days in Gulu, the Lord gave me the opportunity to share with a group of women who called themselves the Daughters of Destiny. This group was comprised of adult women who were there to mentor and be mentored. As I sat and shared with these women what the Lord had given me to bring them that day — the importance of a woman of God knowing and understanding her identity in Christ — my heart literally burned within me. I knew that I had come to Uganda for that purpose. After reluctantly leaving the women due to a tight schedule for that afternoon, I told Robbie, our trip leader, that we needed to chat. I wanted to come back to Uganda and do a retreat for these women. In the States, we have an overabundance of retreats, conferences, concerts, and Bible study choices. Yet the women in Uganda were so hungry for truth, and I wanted to be a part of bringing them the message of hope that God gives us. He was super excited, and I just began to pray and ask that God would show me how to plan through the next year, trusting that He would raise up the right people and resources for this dream.

Just two months later in July, I was given the opportunity to go to Kenya. And when I say given, I mean it. This trip was completely unplanned, at least on my side of things. God knew exactly what He was doing, though. One of my dearest friends, Elissa, called me one day and said, "Do you want to go to Kenya with me in four days?" When Elissa called me that afternoon as I wandered aimlessly around Target, contemplating how I was going to pay for another international trip, she shared with me the one fact that made me say yes. Upon my return from Uganda, Elissa was one of the first people I connected with. We sat down to lunch at The Fickle Pickle, a fun local restaurant, and when I told her about my desire to return to Uganda, she told me all about her friend Jennifer, who is the founder and director of True Identity Ministries[2] — a ministry dedicated to helping men and women find their identity in Christ. Jennifer has done several retreats in the United States and also in Kenya, and she, too was going on this trip and would host a day for women at a pastoral training center just outside of Nairobi. I knew I had to be a part of it. And because God is a God of unspeakable joy and incomprehensible fun, I said yes. He provided all the funds I needed, and I found myself getting myself ready to travel to Africa for the second time in the span of one summer.

Within hours of the conversation with Elissa, I reworked my budget, dipped into my minimal savings, and received gifts from generous friends and family. I ordered more malaria medicine and packed my bags. I was going to Africa. Again. Life with the Lord is a great adventure. Friends and family called me a nomad, Dora the Explorer, and gave looks of disbelief as I recounted to them the Lord's faithfulness in my life and the ways He brought me to the places He knew about before the beginning of time. And I was grateful. Oh so very grateful. While in Uganda, I was busy trying to figure out just what I was there for, and we were running hard. Our trips were long and our days were exhausting.

But in Kenya, I almost felt like I was on a vacation. We stayed at a beautiful campground with the most gorgeous views, and the Lord allowed me so much time with Him that I felt renewed and rejuvenated. The Lord and I had a lot to process through together that summer. In May, I had said goodbye to my friends at the public school I taught at and I was on my way to my dream job at a private Christian school for the inner-city kids of Athens. When I was in Kenya, the summer was beginning to wind down, and I was thinking about all that the fall might entail. I hoped my new surroundings at the school would afford me the chance to meet that man I had been waiting for.

My "tent buddy" or roommate for the week was Jennifer, the True Identity Ministries founder, and we hit it off. We were able to share with one another, and she shared her story with me. I remember her saying she had married in her late twenties and she probably could have waited even longer. I was appalled at the thought of a happily married woman saying that she would have extended her singleness. Wasn't marriage the best thing ever? Why would she ever want to go back to singleness?

As we walked through that week in Kenya, the Lord continued to show me over and over again just how much He loved me by sending me to Africa again in order to know Him more. I watched with delight as women's entire countenances changed after being a part of the True Identity one day conference. These women were set free when they learned of the Father's love, and nothing else mattered to them but His great grace. I wanted their ease of confidence in Christ, and when I returned home, God continued to help me know that He indeed is trustworthy.

By October 2014, I was quite content. I had come to terms with my singleness and was not allowing it to define me. I was blessed to have many amazing friends and a family who loved me unconditionally, and I had been working at my dream job for about three months. Maybe a month prior, I texted my best friend Teresa to tell her that I might lose it if ONE MORE PERSON GOT ENGAGED. But a little while after that, I got myself together, and I recall telling another friend that I was excited and anxious for my love to come along (hopefully sooner rather than later) but that he would "mess up my flow" (Insert crying laughing emoji here!). My routine was busy and I had a lot going on, and I liked it that way.

There were a few little conversations with potential suitors on eHarmony, but nothing ever came to fruition. There were a few guys I talked with for a little bit, but dates were never the result. I admit, I was getting a little discouraged. I mean, I had gone shopping and had a few new pieces that I hoped would be great date items!

It still stung for me to watch so many people pair up, and while I was content, I still had that nagging voice in the back of my mind that said, "When will it be my turn?" It was fun to celebrate others' love stories; heck, I love dancing at weddings! But I still wondered when my turn was coming and if I needed to just get used to being single. I mean, my eHarmony subscription was nearly over! What was I going to do after the subscription ran out? My emotions seemed to be on a yo-yo, and I wanted stability and complete confidence in God.

Lysa Terkeurst writes in her book *Uninvited*,

It's time to stop the lies and devastating hurt stemming from this kind of circumstantial identity. We must tie our identities to our unchanging, unflinching, unyielding, undeniably good, and unquestionably loving God. And the ties that truly bind me to Him and the truth of who I am in Him are given to me in those quiet moments where I say, "I'm Yours, God"... We need to develop an "intimacy-based identity," and this starts with answering three core questions:

- *Is God good?*
- *Is God good to me?*
- *Do I trust God to be God?*

If anyone asked me at that point what I believed about dating, I would have said that I believed in a God who could provide. But I was still waiting on God to just drop a man out of the sky. I wasn't taking any steps toward actually placing myself where that man I so longed for could be. So what did this say about my view of God at that point? It seems like I saw Him as a Santa Claus figure instead of the sovereign and omnipotent God that He is. I hoped that if I was good enough and said all the right prayers, I would lay hold of what He had for me. This theology is oh so skewed. Yes, God is good. Yes, He rewards those who earnestly and diligently seek Him (Hebrews 11:6). Yes, He loves marriage. But He is not a granter of wishes. He is so much more. And when I found myself captivated with God Himself, it was much easier to remember His promises to me.

What I did not realize was that my behavior and actions demonstrated a very different belief than what I professed with my mouth. I said things like "God is in control" and "God will provide," but I was acting as though I believed that "God is in control when He works on my timeline" and "God will provide for everyone but me." When everyone around you is getting what they want, it can be easy to believe the truth for others but not believe it for yourself. God had to remind me over and over and over again that His promises have no expiration date. And the truth is, He doesn't promise marriage to everyone. But He does promise His presence, and I had to trust He was enough. His timeline was often very different than mine, and if I knew all that He knew, I most likely wouldn't change a thing. He was on my side, He was for me, and He was never going to leave me.

One October day, I was on eHarmony and came across a new profile. The user was 28 years old and was in Athens, Georgia! And he seemed normal! Imagine my surprise when I clicked through his profile and found we had a lot in common. I sent him a "wink" and hoped I might hear back soon. Sure enough, we began talking through the steps of guided communication eHarmony provides for its users. Even online, I could see that this guy was different, and it seemed as though we clicked (pun intended). I told my mom and a few friends that I was talking to a "normal, nice, and cute guy" on eHarmony and hoped we would meet one day soon.

Side note here, y'all. The eHarmony site has lots of fun little settings that you can toy with to help your chances of finding someone with whom to connect. I had played around with my geographic settings way too many times, and when I stumbled across this cute guy's profile in Athens, Georgia, I am pretty sure that my settings were NATIONWIDE. I had a couple friends who met their significant other on eHarmony, and the guy moved to the girl's city! At this point, I was ready for anything and hoping for everything, and God was up to something I couldn't fathom or imagine on my own.

On October 6, 2014, I wrote the following entry in my journal:

So this guy Rory on eHarmony. Um. Wow. So kind and so obviously not a boy, but a man. I appreciate his consistency and his kindness. He did a really good job of asking questions that I could make connections to, and I liked that. I just hope I didn't overwhelm him with my answers. Lord, I really like this one. I am so in awe of the really important things that we have in common. And he reads! Ha. Lord, would You help me keep my wits about me in this process? I am getting excited, because it is hard not to be. He is so cute and kind, and I can tell that He loves You.

I have so many fears and reservations about any prospective relationship because all I have for my background experiences are a handful of pseudo-relationships. Lord, I need Your confidence and strength. I need Your wisdom and discernment. Help me to look to You and be found in You. I want to be made more like You in this process. I want to have my heart found within Your heart. Would you show me more of Yourself in this process?

As I think about my time this fall and plans that I've already made, I want to keep my schedule more open for prospective dates. Ha. It is so hard not to let my mind go wandering and imagine all of the fun things we could do here in Athens in the fall. There are so many things I've wanted to do and places I've wanted to go with a boy. So. many. places. And if he's new to Athens, then I could show him these places. I just hope our first date happens within the next couple weeks. I want to be able to talk to Lisa about it in Colorado. I know for sure that I will need her advice.

I have this feeling in my "knower" that this could be the start of something good, but I am afraid to acknowledge it and claim it. I guess by writing it out I just did. Lord, You have my heart.

After about two weeks of talking online, this "normal, nice, and cute guy" named Rory asked if we could take the next step. I flipped the mess out and danced around my room, thrilled that he wanted to meet me in person. Being the inquisitive person that I am (read: stalker), I looked him up on Facebook and after some digging, saw that he attended my church. He called on a Monday evening and asked if we could go to dinner the next night, to which I gladly agreed (Also, can we just give him props for asking me out to dinner on the first date instead of coffee? We both don't even drink coffee anyways, but you get me. Boy has class. I digress.). He also confirmed my suspicions — we went to the same church but had never met. How's that for a God thing?

The next day, I was a bundle of nerves. It was a windy and rainy day in Athens, and I went into school late because there was a severe storm. I remember thinking that if the weather upset my date, I would be devastated. I couldn't eat all day long. Y'all, when I can't eat it means I am either dying or incredibly nervous. All I could think about was this cute guy and whether or not we would hit it off in person.

In the past, I would get overly excited and tell many people about prospective guys in my life. This was my norm because I love people, and I love to talk. It was so fun to dish about a new guy and talk through every little detail of every little conversation. But this guy was different, and this situation seemed different. So I did the best I could to guard everything close to my heart and only shared with my closest friends. Since I'm an extrovert and social butterfly, that was still about 10 people, but you get the picture.

On October 14, 2014, I came home from school and tried to calm myself down, praying the weather would follow suit. The night before I had racked my brain for what to wear, and I decided on my favorite chambray dress with boots. Dressy casual, I'd say. After taking a shower, painting my nails, and meticulously doing my makeup, I left in plenty of time (also highly uncharacteristic of me since I am always late.) I drove around downtown Athens, just hoping I could find a parking spot near Ted's Most Best, a local restaurant where we had agreed to meet. When I pulled into my spot, a couple minutes later, Rory pulled up next to me. We both got out of the car and then walked to the restaurant together. Little did I know that my life would be forever changed because of that first meeting.

Chapter 9

So, This is Love

Because he bends down to listen, I will pray as long as I have breath! - Psalm 116:2 (NLT)

I remember being so worried about whether or not Rory and I would have anything to talk about on our first date. Of course, I had told a few of my friends and my family about him, so there were a handful of people who knew that we would be meeting that evening. My phone buzzed with well wishes when I was on the way, and then I put it on "Do Not Disturb" mode so that I would not be distracted throughout the evening. After writing back and forth for two weeks about most of the topics covered on a first date, I wondered if we would have much to say to each other. Did we already say everything that could be said?! Much to my surprise, Rory and I did not lack for conversation topics; in fact, we talked for almost two and a half hours. We covered several different topics — our jobs, our families, our interests, our dreams — the conversation definitely flowed! I made our goodbye a little awkward when I went in for a full hug, but he was gracious about it and didn't hold it against me.

After our first date, I was pretty smitten with Rory. I wanted so badly to talk to him and see him again. I was so interested in his life and his story; I wanted to know everything about him! He was so kind and gentle, and there was a quiet and strong confidence about him that was so attractive and endearing to me. We started texting a little bit throughout the week, and then that weekend I ran the Athens half marathon (my last half marathon since meeting him, #goodbyerunning) and had many other social engagements. Rory promised he would check in and see when we could meet up again, and I knew he would be true to his word.

Rory and I were able to go on a few more dates before I took a trip to Colorado to see some of my dearest friends from Mexico. I remember being so excited to see them and to talk with Lisa, my friend and mentor, about him, but also so sad to leave him because I was truly enjoying getting to know him. While I was away, I missed him terribly. I remember feeling a physical longing to be where he was. It was so strange, and I actually wondered what was wrong with me! I read my friend Gretchen Saffles' book *A God-Sized Love Story[1]* on the plane on the way there and cried and prayed for this exciting new possibility.

On October 27, 2014, I wrote these words in my journal:

Lord, I simply cannot believe how quickly my life seems to be changing. I am just so undone. It seems crazy because it hasn't even been a full two weeks with Rory, but already everything just feels so different in a good way. In the best way. And I love that. I love that we are so very different in some ways and yet the same in the most important ways. Thank you for that, Lord. I kind of feel like I am going crazy or like I am going to bust out of my skin when I am not with him. I've never been able to talk to a guy so easily without flirting or putting on airs. And I am so so grateful for that. It sounds crazy, and I am not telling another soul, but I want to marry this man. I do. I love his quiet confidence. I love his heart for other people. I love his sincerity. And I love the way he leads and pursues me. I'm not left guessing. And that is so very refreshing. Lord, thank you so much for this gift. Help me to just enjoy it and continue to have a heart of gratitude.

When I returned home from my trip to Colorado, Rory was sick with a cold. I was disappointed to have to wait to see him, but when he got better, we pretty much became inseparable. We went on fun dates around our town - trying new restaurants, taking lots of walks, and talking. Always talking. In November, I was able to meet his sister and her husband, and we finally had the dreaded "DTR" conversation. It was time to Define The Relationship. I had been hoping and praying I wouldn't have to bring it up, but I just really wanted some clarity. In my heart, I knew that he was made for me, but I didn't have any way of knowing what his true thoughts and feelings were for me. We were on our way to his sister's house for a Friends-giving meal, and I thought to myself, It's now or never! So, I turned to him in the car and said, "So when we get to your sister's house, how are you going to introduce me? I mean, am I your friend or your girlfriend?"

Rory didn't skip a beat and said, "I mean, I consider you my girlfriend. Is that okay with you?"

"Is that okay? I already know I'm going to marry you, boy!" I replied.

Okay, so I didn't really say that, but something close to that was running through my mind! I quickly agreed, and I remember thinking (with joy) how weird it was that I could finally say I had a boyfriend! After that, I think I had a perma-grin. Nobody could wipe the smile off of my face! Right before Thanksgiving, Rory was able to meet my students. Prior to this, we talked with one another about the elephant in the room — the fact that he is white and I am black. One night, we went to the UGA intramural fields to hang out, but it was so cold that we ended up in his car just talking. There was a lull in conversation, and then he said to me, "So, how do your parents feel about the fact that you're dating a white guy?"

I replied, "Oh, they don't care. As long as you love Jesus. What do your parents say?"

"Oh, my parents don't mind," he stated with confidence. "My mom has always wanted mixed grandbabies."

So. There you have it, folks. He was already talking about our children! We were in this thing for the long haul, and we hadn't even said, "I love you!"

When Rory first came to the school I taught at, the story was a little different. My entire class was comprised of African-American students who are not often surrounded by people who look different from them. As we sat at the table for our Thanksgiving luncheon, my student Jamal said incredulously, "He's your boyfriend? Ew, that's weird because of your colors!" Rory replied without hesitation, "It's ok, that doesn't matter." He's always cool as a cucumber. I, however, was mortified and wanted to crawl under the table.

The weekend before Thanksgiving proved to be a big one for us. Not only did Rory meet my kids, but I met his parents! I was somewhat nervous and didn't know how we would get along, but we went to a Mexican restaurant and had so much fun. His mom and I bonded over our love for dystopian young adult fiction, and I knew we would be friends. After meeting his parents, we drove back to Rory's apartment, and it was time for me to head off for Thanksgiving break. As we sat in the car, I said, "I really like your family. They are so sweet!"

To which he replied, "Well, they're crazy about you, and I am, too."

HEART SOARING

CHEEKS FLUSHING

IS THIS REAL LIFE?!

But friend, it got even better, because when Rory walked me over to my car to say goodbye, we hugged for a long time, and then he gave me my very first kiss! It was probably more like a lip brushing, and in the minutes following, I wondered whether it had even happened, but it had! I was on cloud nine. I could barely drive and had to pull over into a grocery store parking lot to call my mom. Then, when I arrived at my friend Ali's apartment where I was having a girl's night, I busted into the apartment by screaming, "GUESS WHO JUST GOT KISSED?!""Life could have stopped for me right there, and I probably would have died the happiest girl on earth.

After spending the night with my friends, I went home to Marietta for the week of Thanksgiving, and Rory and I just about died from separation anxiety. We had grown accustomed to seeing each other nearly every day, and it seemed so strange to not be with each other! When he was finally able to make his way from Athens to Marietta, Rory then met my parents, which went well. I think he was a little overwhelmed, because the Miller clan is much louder and expressive than his family. But somehow, he managed to keep up with the conversations and was able to get a stamp of approval from my parents. And as the cherry on top, before we said goodbye and he headed back home to be with his family, he told me he loved me. I had been thinking the same thing for a few weeks, so of course I said it back.

I absolutely could not believe what was happening to me. Everything I had prayed about for years was finally coming to fruition, and it almost seemed too good to be true. And it was all happening so fast. In the span of two short months, I had met the man I was going to marry and we had declared our love for each other. I wanted to slow down time and bottle up every single precious moment. During my singleness, many friends often tried to comfort me by reminding me of how God's timeline is often different than our own. This quip was particularly difficult for me to hear, and it was not always comforting. Had I done something wrong to make God "late?" Why wasn't He giving me what I wanted now? As I prayed and begged and prayed some more during my singleness, the Lord constantly reminded me of His goodness. He gave me His perspective and allowed me to grow in gratitude for all that He was doing in my life in the present moment instead of constantly pining for the future.

But there is something to be said for the prayers I prayed and the God who answered them. There were many precious friends in my life who told me they were praying for my future spouse, and I believe that God answered their prayers and my own. In the book of Genesis, we see one of the most idyllic love stories in the Bible as a father's prayers are answered. Isaac and Rebekah's story is one for the Hollywood screens. We already know that God promised to make Abraham a father of many nations. In order to be a father of many nations, Abraham would need many descendants. And in order to make descendants, Abraham would need for his children to find spouses! But these spouses couldn't be just anyone. They needed to be the right fit if they were to be in his family line.

Abraham knew the importance of maintaining purity within the family line, so in his old age, he sent his servant on perhaps the greatest mission he'd ever been entrusted with - the search for the perfect daughter-in-law. No pressure, right? Abraham's servant set out on a journey to Nahor, knowing he would only be successful with the Lord's help. He sought the Lord and asked him for favor, and the Lord showed up in a way that only He could. Let's take a look at this story in Genesis 24:

Then the servant took ten of his master's camels and departed, taking all sorts of choice gifts from his master; and he arose and went to Mesopotamia to the city of Nahor. And he made the camels kneel down outside the city by the well of water at the time of evening, the time when women go out to draw water. And he said, "O Lord, God of my master Abraham, please grant me success today and show steadfast love to my master Abraham. Behold, I am standing by the spring of water, and the daughters of the men of the city are coming out to draw water. Let the young woman to whom I shall say, 'Please let down your jar that I may drink" and who shall say, 'Drink, and I will water your camels' — let her be the one whom you have appointed for your servant Isaac. By this I shall know that you have shown steadfast love to my master."

Before he had finished speaking, behold, Rebekah, who was born to Bethuel the son of Milcah, the wife of Nahor, Abraham's brother, came out with her water jar on her shoulder. The young woman was very attractive in appearance, a maiden whom no man had known. She went down to the spring and filled her jar and came up. Then the servant ran to meet her and said, "Please give me a little water to drink from your jar." She said, "Drink, my lord." And she quickly let down her jar upon her hand and gave him a drink. When she had finished giving him a drink, she said, "I will draw water for your camels also, until they have finished drinking." So she quickly emptied her jar into the trough and ran again to the well to draw water, and she drew for all his camels. The man gazed at her in silence to learn whether the Lord had prospered his journey or not.

When the camels had finished drinking, the man took a gold ring weighing a half shekel, and two bracelets for her arms weighing ten gold shekels, and said, "Please tell me whose daughter you are. Is there room in your father's house for us to spend the night?" She said to him, "I am the daughter of Bethuel the son of Milcah, whom she bore to Nahor." She

added, "We have plenty of both straw and fodder, and room to spend the night." The man bowed his head and worshiped the Lord and said, "Blessed be the Lord, the God of my master Abraham, who has not forsaken his steadfast love and his faithfulness toward my master. As for me, the Lord has led me in the way to the house of my master's kinsmen."
Genesis 24:10-27

Friend, is the overwhelming lovingkindness of God as obvious to you as it is to me? In this passage, we witness the sovereignty of God. How many women could have come to draw water? How many seemingly inconsequential decisions led Rebekah to draw water on that day? Do you think she had any idea how her life would change from one simple decision? Abraham's servant took seriously the mission bestowed upon him, and because of his sincerity, his prayers were answered and God's glory shown for everyone to see. Verse 15 says, "Before he had finished speaking, behold Rebekah...came out with her water jar on her shoulder" (emphasis mine).

Before he had finished speaking, God answered his prayer. Before he had arrived to town, God orchestrated every little detail of their meeting. Before the beginning of time, God knew both how He would bring Isaac and Rebekah together and the exact circumstances of their love story. Before anyone else knew how the line of Abraham would be established, God knew. It was God's idea to bless Abraham, and it was His plan to bring it to fruition in a way that would astound not only his servant but all of Abraham's family. You see, it is easy to think that God is silent when our prayers are not answered in our timing and to our specifications. But we have to remember that God is the God of immeasurably more.

Then Rebekah and her young women arose and rode on the camels and followed the man. Thus the servant took Rebekah and went his way.

Now Isaac had returned from Beer-lahai-roi and was dwelling in the Negeb. And Isaac went out to meditate in the field toward evening. And he lifted up his eyes and saw, and behold, there were camels coming. And Rebekah lifted up her eyes, and when she saw Isaac, she dismounted from the camel

and said to the servant, "Who is that man, walking in the field to meet us?" The servant said, "It is my master." So she took her veil and covered herself. And the servant told Isaac all the things that he had done. Then Isaac brought her into the tent of Sarah his mother and took Rebekah, and she became his wife, and he loved her. So Isaac was comforted after his mother's death.
-Genesis 24:61-67

In His omniscience, God is weaving together the perfect tapestry for every person's story. And He knows that every single bit of it is good. The waiting, the longing, and the yearning — all of these parts are good. Because when we remember that He hears our every cry, we are encouraged to sit in the waiting and allow Him to do what He does best — be God. Rebekah and Isaac have a "love at first sight" moment and are captivated by one another. God in His kindness allows them to fall in love with one another and see each other through eyes of adoration.

In December 2014, I wrote the following in my journal:

It is absolutely crazy to me to think about how much my life has changed in the last two months. I have been hoping and praying for this change for so long, and now that it is here I am so very overcome by emotion. I feel very raw, vulnerable, and afraid — afraid of the unknown and of messing it up. These are such intense feelings that I have, and I am afraid because I know that feelings can change and can be fickle...

Lord, I love Rory so much that is scares me. It simultaneously relieved and terrified me to hear him say that he is in this for the long haul. I feel the same way, and it blows my mind to think that I could know someone for two months and know that I want to spend the rest of my life with him. I know that right now things are good and new and exciting, and I am aware that they will not always be this way. I want to remember this feeling, though. I always want to remember that I am actively choosing Rory. I am choosing to love all of him, and I do not want to ever forget that.

70

Lord, would you continue to hold my heart? Would You help me to be present in the moment when I am with Rory? Help me to know how to love him without holding on too tightly. Help me to trust You, Lord. I cannot trust You in my own strength. I can only run to You when I am weak, worried, and prone to wander. Show me how to react in Your arms.

I continued to lay down my burdens at the foot of the cross. They say that change — even good change — is difficult, and they're right, because processing through these emotions and through the newness of this relationship was challenging for me as everything happened so quickly! But the Lord was so sweet and gracious to me as I walked in the midst of this whirlwind relationship. The rest of 2014 was so fun and full of sweet memories as Rory and I continued to get to know one another. He was able to slowly meet many of my close friends, and I met his college friends during Christmas break. I kept the treasures of this sweet relationship close to my heart as I knew that this was the start of something new. There was no going back now! My life had completely changed, just like Rebekah's when she was brought to Isaac. At the start of 2015, I knew I wanted to be married that year. You know what they say: when you know, you know.

Chapter 10

When You Know, You Know

I lift up my eyes to the hills.
From where does my help come?
My help comes from the Lord,
who made heaven and earth.
- Psalm 121:1

As a single 20-something with little to no dating experience, I remember wondering how I would know when I met my husband. Would it be some incredible feeling? Would sparks fly? How would I know when God brought along the man with whom I was to spend all of my days? I remember friends and mentors saying, "When you know, you know." That little quip wasn't much help to someone who wants to be in control and have all the answers right away. Patience is not exactly my strong suit, and it was killing me to not have a concrete way to know. A writing in the sky or a letter in the mail would be great, thank you very much.

During this time of waiting and wondering, my Jesus became so very dear to me. I journaled almost daily as I processed all of my thoughts and feelings. It was a practice that was quite cathartic and much needed. I'd never fallen in love before, and everything within and around me felt like it was spinning out of control.

As I reflected on how my life was beginning to change, I went back to "The List." As I reviewed the characteristics I had prayed over for the past three years, I found myself weeping, because Rory fulfilled each and every one of them.
- He was a good listener, because he never cut me off or seemed bored when we talked together. In fact, he said he liked it

when I talked! As someone who had been known as a big talker for the majority of her life, this was a huge encouragement to my insecure heart.

- He was compassionate and generous, because he moved to the Athens area to help take care of a family member in a time of need. Who does that? When I read that on eHarmony, I knew he was for me.
- He conformed to God and not the world, because he cared more about serving and helping others than advancing his own name.
- He was dependable, because he always checked in on me and did what he said he would do.
- He had a great sense of humor and made me laugh so easily.
- He was humble, because he never liked to draw attention to himself. His humility is unmatched and is still one of my very favorite things about him.
- He was obedient, because he wanted to do things God's way.
- He was pure, because he wanted us to pursue God's best and never did things with a self-advancing motive.
- He was sincere, because he was the same person in every situation.
- He trusted God's timing, because he didn't care if our story was different from others'; it was ours.

Now to him who is able to do immeasurably more than all we ask or imagine, according to his power that is at work within us, to him be glory in the church and in Christ Jesus throughout all generations, for ever and ever! Amen. - Ephesians 3:20-21 (NIV)

When the Lord led me to Rory, I truly found my "immeasurably more." I had just about given up hope and thought maybe men like him didn't exist. I figured I would be single for a while and maybe I had heard the Lord wrong when I thought He had promised me a husband. But I hadn't, and in His perfect timing, He provided the perfect man for me.

Rory and I met on October 14, 2014. He told me he loved me the day before Thanksgiving, and we were talking about marriage shortly after. I remember riding in the car on the way back from our first road trip together at the beginning of 2015 and asking him about how he'd like his life to look different within the next year. He responded, "Well, if things are still going well with us, I think we could be engaged by this time next year." My heart sank within me. Engaged?! Within a year? I was thinking we could be married in 2015! Cue panic mode. Fortunately, later that day, he changed his tune and said, "You know what? I think we could be married this year. This is our year." Phew! That was a close one!

Once we decided it was going to happen within that year, I prayed all the more, and the Lord pressed July on my heart. I didn't know why, I just figured why wait? We weren't in our young twenties, waiting on college graduation or job security. We knew what we wanted and we knew we loved each other. Plus, I was still teaching elementary school at the time. I didn't want to get married during Thanksgiving or Christmas break, and summer just seemed to make the most sense. It took a bit of prayer and convincing on Rory's part; he wanted to be able to get me a nice ring and do things right. But by February, we had decided on July. I began daydreaming about what the perfect proposal would look like and thinking about what it would be like to finally wear a ring on my left hand.

It was April 2015, and Rory and I had been planning a trip to the beach for about a month. We were watching the television show Parks and Recreation one night, and the episode where Andy and April spontaneously drive to the Grand Canyon and camp out in their car inspired us. Obviously, we couldn't drive to the Grand Canyon too easily from Athens, Georgia, but nevertheless, we were inspired. We have a bucket list to which we're always adding adventures we want to have, places we want to go, and things we want to do. So, the beach trip to see the sunrise was going to check off one of our sights — either Charleston or Savannah.

As the day got closer, I just had this feeling that Rory would propose. I knew that when we went, it would be days away from our six-month anniversary. We talked about how we wanted a short engagement. We had gone ring shopping, and we already had a venue, date and time chosen for the ceremony. It seemed like half the wedding was already planned. The only thing missing was the ring to make it official! All the signs were pointing to a proposal on that special day. I told my mom what I was thinking, but I didn't tell anyone else for fear of being wrong. Throughout the week, people asked me if I thought I knew when he would

74

propose, but I didn't tell anyone what I hoped would happen on that Saturday morning.

On Friday night, we both went to bed uncharacteristically early, around eight o'clock. It felt so strange to go to bed while anticipating that I would be getting up in the middle of the night. I had a little bag with a change of clothes and road trip snacks, and I was ready. A little after one in the morning, I got up (I hadn't really been sleeping anyways) and pulled on my yoga pants and my "prophetic tee shirt," which reads, THE BEST IS YET TO COME.

Ror came and picked me up around two in the morning, and we were on our way. The ride down was easy and smooth; we talked and listened to music and comedians to keep us awake. I took a little nap and continued to pray that the weather would stay nice and not get yucky so we could have a good day. We got to Tybee Island around 6:30 in the morning, just in time for the sunrise at 7:00 a.m. Ror had a little gym bag he brought with him to the beach, and I was hoping there was a little something special in it for me. He had mentioned that he had some surprises for the morning, so my hopes were up!

We got to the beach and put our things down on a swing. He opened up his gym bag, and he had a sweet surprise — Chinese lanterns. We previously talked about how we wanted to include them in our wedding but wouldn't be able to because of our venue location (yes we chose and booked the venue before we got engaged, it's fine), so we lit them that morning and watched them float away above the ocean. We watched the lanterns drift until we could no longer see them, and then we took our blanket down closer to the water and laid down for a little bit.

At this point, I was hoping for and expecting the proposal, but I so badly did not want to be wrong. I was staring out at the ocean, just praying that the Lord would help me to have a good attitude if it didn't happen that day and to enjoy the special trip we took together. After what seemed like an eternity, Rory sat up and told me that he had a special gift for our six-month anniversary, even though it was a few days away. Of course, I told him I wanted it right then. He pulled a stack of journals out of his bag, and in my mind, I thought, "Oh my. Where's the ring? I hope we didn't drive for four hours for him to give me journals. I mean I love journals, but seriously?!"

I pretty much put them aside and looked at him expectantly, and then he asked me to actually look inside one of the journals. And that's when the mini freak-out commenced. He had made the sweetest scrapbook entitled "Our Firsts" with pictures and dates of all our milestones: first date, first road trip, first kiss, etc. And on the very last page, it said: "Engagement Day" with that day's date (which just happened to be exactly three months from our wedding day). In the back of the journal, Rory had glued all of the pages together and then carved out a hole where he put the ring on a string. I was floored and so taken aback by his thoughtfulness and creativity, knowing it doesn't come naturally to him to be "crafty." Plus, I was freaking out and wanted to see the ring. Duh. As soon as I saw it, I just kept saying, "Oh my gosh! Oh my gosh! Oh my gosh!

Rory took the ring out of the journal and said a bunch of sweet and wonderful things, and then he asked me to marry him. I enthusiastically said "Yes, yes, yes!" and kissed him, and then we sat and stared at the ring together. Right after he asked, the sun started to peek through the clouds, and we took it as a sign that the Lord was pleased with our upcoming nuptials. I called my parents, and he texted his. Everyone was super excited and knew it was coming. This all happened before eight in the morning, so it was quite the day. I was so excited and wanted to tell the world, but we spent the day together by going to breakfast and seeing special places around Savannah before getting in touch with all of our friends.

Overall, our proposal day was one of the sweetest days, and I honestly couldn't believe that it was all finally happening. It was finally my turn, and in three short months, my last name and my entire life were going to change. Now, at this point, I was still questioning how all of this could be happening to me. How in the world was I engaged when six months prior I barely knew this guy? How was I going to plan a wedding in three short months? Would I be able to get everything done in time?

For those who live according to the flesh set their minds on the things of the flesh, but those who live according to the Spirit set their minds on the things of the Spirit. For to set the mind of the flesh is death, but to set the mind on the Spirit is life and peace. For the mind that is set on the flesh is hostile to God, for it does not submit to God's law; indeed, it cannot. Those are in the flesh cannot please God. - Romans 8:5-8

Friend, I'm going to be 100% honest with you and tell you that this was an ugly time of the heart for me. Engagement was one of the hardest seasons of my life. This season is a time in which you are preparing to be one with your future spouse. But the hardest part is that you're not one yet. You're living in an in-between time in which you feel like you're married in just about every sense of the word, but you're not quite there. And that, my friend, is one of the most difficult things there is. If you're willing to be real with your future spouse, then during engagement some things are beginning to surface that were not there before. You're beginning to face some of your flaws and tendencies. You're deciding whether you want to be right or be kind.

As stated before, I was the bridesmaid many times — six to be exact — before walking down the aisle to my own Prince Charming. So, when it was my turn, there were certain expectations I had about how things should be and what I believed I deserved. And what's amazing about it is that many people applauded this behavior. The world has told us that the wedding is all about the bride and it's ok (and expected) for her to lose her mind during engagement and turn into a complete bridezilla. And yet the world — as usual — is so completely wrong in this way of thinking.

When I was planning our wedding, I thought about all that God had done and the ways He had provided for me to bring me to the place I was as a new fiancé. I couldn't believe His provision and His perfect timing. I thought about how I wanted our wedding to be a reflection of His goodness and all that He did in sending His Son through whom we have life and salvation. This wedding was going to be all about Jesus, not about me, the bride.

Yet the temptation to feed the "me monster" was so real. I didn't want people to have an opinion on things, and I didn't want people to ask me a ton of "annoying" questions. I just wanted to get to the wedding day and be done with it. But. Just as God doesn't hand new parents a 12-year-old and say, "Good luck," He doesn't expect us to transition from one life stage to another without some degree of difficulty, especially when we don't fully and completely rely on Him.

On June 22, 2015, just weeks before the wedding, I wrote in my journal:

I absolutely cannot believe that I am getting married in 19 days. My entire life has been leading up to this point. It is almost madness to think about the fact that one year ago today, I did not know Rory Alexander Mathisen existed. I had no idea I would be engaged a year later. Oh, how quickly things can change! The Lord is so good, and His timing is so, so perfect. Lord, thank You for Rory. Thank You for the way You provide. Thank You for Your grace. Thank You for Your kindness. Thank You for Your goodness. Thank You for Your faithfulness.

Engagement was a hard but necessary time. Over and over I had to remind myself that I was choosing Rory. I wasn't choosing appetizers, playlists, and bridesmaid dress colors. I was choosing Rory. And because I was choosing to unite my life to his, it would never be the same. The enemy, however, knows our fragility and sees when we are vulnerable. There were so many attacks on me mentally and emotionally, and as I began to question everything. Was I crazy to be marrying someone I barely knew? How much did I really know about this man? What if he changed after we got married? What if I wasn't happy all the time? What if? What if? What if?

Be watchful, stand firm in the faith, act like men, be strong.
Let all that you do be done in love.
-1 Corinthians 16:13-14

I must confess to you it was immensely difficult for me to stand firm during this season. So much so that I questioned whether or not I was making the right decision. No one talks about how you wonder if you truly love the person you're going to marry. No one talks about the fears that present themselves when you're making the single most important decision of your life. The enemy is very cunning, my friend. He wants to twist anything that God has said is good. He wants to take the truth of God's word and use it against you. He does not want you to walk in wholeness.

No matter how much I struggled or how far I strayed, by running past boundaries or hurting people close to me, God never stopped pursuing me. So even in the midst of fear, I knew that Rory was the man God had for me. In the midst of fear, I knew that God had been preparing me through my whole life for such a time as this. In the midst of fear, I knew that God was still going to shine brightly, regardless of my anxieties, hang-ups, and failures.

There's a reason why people are usually engaged for longer than three months. I still wouldn't change our timeline, but wow was there a lot to process in such a short amount of time! There is much to be said for loving the process and for allowing God to work in and through you as He sanctifies and prepares you for His plan for your life. But there is also much to be said for His unending grace in the midst of change, uncertainty, and transition. He is the same God yesterday, today, and forever. And for that, I am truly grateful.

Chapter 11

The Covenant

Give thanks to the Lord, for He is good, for His steadfast love endures forever. - Psalm 136:1

Before we got married, it was easy to focus on the wedding. We knew that the wedding would be one fleeting day that would come and go all too quickly. Marriage, however, is for the long haul. And so we prepared, as best as we could, for marriage and our lives together after the day full of pomp and circumstance. Planning a wedding is often seen as a stressful endeavor, and it certainly can be. But the beauty in the midst of the chaos is that you are uniting your life with someone else's. You are no longer on your own, and life as you know it has completely changed. You will be forever yoked to your best friend. That's simultaneously exciting yet terrifying, am I right?

As I prepared for the wedding, I often had to pinch myself and could not believe that I had the privilege of leading the life I was living. It seemed surreal to finally be the bride after being the bridesmaid so many times. And the wonderful thing was that there were so many people who were excited about us falling in love! I got to have showers and receive gifts and wear a pretty dress, all because the Lord had brought me my beloved! It seemed too good to be true!

The weeks leading up to the wedding were extremely busy and full. We went on a vacation with Rory's college friends to the beach over the fourth of July holiday weekend, and when we returned, we had the joy of moving into our first apartment. I am ever the optimist and figured it would take us about half a day. Boy, was I wrong! Because I was on summer break from teaching, I had been sorting, cleaning, and purging through all of the belongings in the house I shared with my roommate. Rory was still working full time and had done as much as he could, but let's just say there was much to be done that Monday morning. That day proved to be over 12 hours of moving, and we were exhausted. It proved to be a wonderful test of our love for one another when we were not at our best. There's nothing like moving to bring out your true colors!

Once we had our apartment, it began to seem much more real. Even though I was staying at a friend's house until the wedding, Rory lived at the apartment for the two weeks leading up to the wedding. Each day, I went over to unpack our gifts and set up our very first home. At this point, I was so ready to be out of the engagement season and to have two rings on my left hand and a new name. The process to get to the wedding day was certainly not easy, and I was so grateful that July 11, 2015 was just around the corner.

A couple weeks after our wedding, I wrote the following on my blog:

> It is hard to believe that our wedding day has come and gone. Everyone told me that it would go quickly and that the day would be a blur, but I tried to stay present throughout the day and remember the special faces and moments that I know we will treasure forever. We could not have imagined a better day and are so grateful to everyone who attended our wedding, prayed from afar, and supported us through the engagement season. There are so many people who worked together and prayed over our day, and the beauty of the time we spent celebrating what God had done to bring us together and begin our journey as one was overwhelming. There were a few moments that were just breathtaking — walking down the aisle to Rory waiting for me, having our wedding party and parents pray over us, and walking into the reception hall knowing that all of our closest friends and family had come together that day to celebrate us.
>
> Our prayer was that our ceremony would be intimate and worshipful. We wanted God to be glorified and for

people to know the purpose of marriage — to paint a picture of Christ and His church. On that day, when we took communion together, the sun broke out through the windows of the chapel, and it was a beautiful testimony of the light of Christ that we hold in our hearts and pray shines through us to draw others unto Him.

Rory and I wrote our own vows to one another, and every time I look at them and think about them, I remember that these are promises we made not only to each other, but to our Heavenly Father. We are not perfect, and there is no way we will completely fulfill each one of these promises each day. But He gives us the grace to love and serve each other each day, and as we cling to Him, we grow closer and slowly begin to understand the depths of His wonderful love.

Our Vows

I, Jessica Nicole, vow before the Lord and these witnesses to give you myself fully today.
I promise to remember that Christ is my first love and you are my beloved.
I promise to do you good and not harm all the days of my life.
I promise to encourage you and remember that we are better together.
I promise to serve you with a cheerful heart and laugh with you at the times to come.
I promise to listen to you with understanding and cherish each day the Lord gives us.
I promise to respect you and submit to your leadership by remembering that you are always for me.
I promise to love you unconditionally and to pursue peace as we journey through God's adventure for us.
You are my promise fulfilled, my dream come true, and my best friend.

I, Rory Alexander, vow to give all of myself to you today.
I promise to be faithful to you always and to keep Christ as the center of our marriage at all times.
I promise to love you unconditionally and to guide and protect your heart as long as we are both alive.

I promise to always be honest with you and to be a true and honest friend.
I promise to pray with you each morning and each night and to keep myself immersed in God's word.
I promise to laugh with you in times of joy, grieve with you in times of sorrow, and grow with you in love as we serve the world together.
I promise to listen to all of your thoughts, your hopes, your fears, and your dreams as well as share with you mine.
And I promise to respect you, encourage you, and cherish you as I continue to try and become worthy of your love.
You are my best friend and the love of my life, and today you become my crown.

It is crazy how fast you can forsake the vows you made to your beloved before God and your closest friends and family. Everything seems so perfect on the wedding day as you are surrounded by your nearest and dearest loved ones. The dress, the flowers, the hair, the food, the dancing...it's all gone according to plan, so why shouldn't the rest of your lives together? In all honesty, it quickly became evident that it was going to take a whole lot of Jesus for us to truly enjoy being around each other for the rest of our lives.

With a whirlwind romance finally coming to a standstill, my emotions were everywhere. My life had completely changed, and while I was present for the whole thing, I felt like someone had just plopped me in the middle of a movie I'd never seen before. The realities of living every single day with my new husband quickly threw me for a loop. There were so many surprises and things that I didn't realize would rattle me like they did. I didn't realize I would feel like my whole identity was changing. It seems melodramatic to say, but I was so shaken by the fact that my life would never be the same. This thought once thrilled me, but now I was just plain scared.

There was nothing wrong, and we hadn't rushed into anything, even though we had only known each other for nine months at this point. It was just that the amount of change we went through in that brief time would be difficult for anyone to handle. We both had expectations we brought into our marriage, and it was easy to look to the other person to fulfill the dreams and fantasies that were entertained about marriage before we even met. We could have said to one another, "I'm not relying on you for my happiness," but our attitudes often suggested otherwise.

Marriage is one of those things people have a slew of opinions about — some good and some, well, not so good. Before we got married, people were telling me all kinds of things. This whirlwind romance invited all sorts of words of wisdom from nearly everyone in my life. It was almost like we were supposed to be scared about marriage because it was going to be the biggest change ever, and we were going to be feeling all sorts of feelings and learning all sorts of things. And to that I say, yes. I was feeling all sorts of feelings and learning all sorts of things. But it was good. It was really good.

Rory and I had the conversation several times about why we think so many people told us marriage would be hard. Is it because they were really young when they married and had to "grow up" together? Do they just like drama? Are we supposed to be fighting more?! There are myriad ways to look at marriage. We choose to look at it in a Biblical sense. Marriage is a covenant between a man, a woman, and God. It is not to be taken lightly and is a portrait of the church as the bride of Christ. Marriage can depict true love to the world when two people commit to daily dying to their wants and choosing to live for someone else's ultimate good.

People often say that we have to "trust the process." And to that saying I give one hundred million yeses and amens. Here's the thing though: I do not like trusting the process. No ma'am, I do not! Give me immediate results. Give me what I want and need (or what I think I need) on my timeline, please and thank you. The college pastor at our church often tells students, "We serve a crockpot God in a microwave world." Sounds silly, but we do not want to go through the sanctification process. We want to be made more like Christ, but we do not want to go through the often painful steps it takes to get there. We want to be holy but are unwilling to confront our sin and be vulnerable before others in order to experience genuine life change. Marriage is one of the most sanctifying tools there is. Living daily life with someone and working through hard things instead of stuffing them or sweeping them under the rug is a choice. Sometimes it is a difficult choice, but it is always the best choice.

Here's the thing: marriage is hard. There, I said it. But you know what? Life is hard. I think we need to shift our thinking about life in general, not just marriage. Hard does not equal bad. Easy does not equal good. The circumstances and life stages we deem the most difficult are what God will use to mold and shape us. And on the other side of those trials, we oftentimes say we would not have it any other way. When we have an eternal perspective, we are able to see the beauty in the tapestry that God is weaving in each of our lives. So when I see my sin before me for the umpteenth time and am reminded of my selfishness, do I get upset and whine that this marriage thing is hard and I want out? Or do I thank God for continuing to sanctify me and making me more like His Son? I've found when my attitude changes regarding a circumstance, the circumstance does not usually change. But when my attitude changes, I become more moldable and willing in the hands of a God who's not finished with me yet. I am lighter and can rest easy when I know that my attitude honors the Lord.

People get married for all sorts of reasons. Some people get married hoping they will no longer be lonely. Others marry for hopes of financial stability. Still others marry because they want a family of their own someday. So let's pull back the curtain a little bit and take the time to examine our hearts. I am convinced that marriages that do not thrive are in danger because of the lack of vulnerability and honesty within this sacred covenant relationship. The same can be said for individuals. If we are not daring to live with vulnerability and honesty before at least one other person in this world, how can we grow and offer our best selves to the world?

We must remember that a Christian marriage is unlike any other relationship on earth. When two Christ-followers come together, they are saying to the other, "Where you go I go. Where you are is my home. Your good is more important to me than anything else. My life is forever united with yours." A covenant marriage is not about getting what you want or like a business transaction. A covenant marriage is about dying to yourself and your ways every. single. day. A covenant marriage is not to be respected and honored when you feel like it. It's for life.

Yes, marriage is hard, but it is also the best gift I have ever been given. Not only is Rory the best speaker of truth over me, swatting down the enemy's lies like the spiritual leader ninja he is, he is also just really funny. We laugh about the dumbest things. Like, I think we are 10 years old sometimes! We have so much fun. So while communication is hard and awkward sometimes, and I whine about silly things, this marriage thing is also really, really fun. For real, y'all. There's nothing better than coming home every day knowing that your best friend will be there.

We got married because we love each other and we love the Lord. He brought us together, and we love that fact. We believe we are better together than apart and that our personalities and gifts work together to make one pretty great person. We were both doing just fine before we got married; we were whole. Neither of us "completes" the other. Because here's the thing about marriage: it shows you sides of yourself you most likely haven't seen and wouldn't have seen otherwise. Sometimes this is painful, at least when you resist it. But when you realize that the Lord gave you this person to walk alongside forever, then you are immensely grateful and do not want to imagine life without them. And the beauty is that my strengths are his weaknesses, and his strengths are my weaknesses. Funny how perfect God's provision is, isn't it?

I could live my life without Rory. I shudder to think about what it would be like, because he enriches my life daily and encourages me. He strengthens me and cheers me on, and he takes care of me. Plus, he's incredibly handsome and it's pretty great to wake up next to him every morning! But I could live life without him. He's not Jesus. Here's the thing, though: I don't want to live my life without him. I love him beyond words. He is my best friend, my confidante, and my home. So I chose not to live life without him when I took his name, knowing my life would never be the same. And each day, until death parts us or Jesus Christ returns, I will keep on choosing him. Because it's worth it.

Chapter 12

Our Covenant God

Oh, the Covenant, that we are living in
It's more than rings on hands
It's a yes to the unknown
And in seasons of drought
Or when famine comes around
We go to the storehouse
To the One who is always faithful
- Bethany Barnard, "Covenant"

We don't speak of covenants often in our culture, but in Biblical times, a covenant was a well-known part of culture and a serious thing. In the Old Testament, God required the priests to offer perfect sacrifices in order to atone for their sins and the sins of the people. In the Old Testament, we also read prophecy after prophecy of how God was going to send a perfect sacrifice that would atone for all of our sin, once and for all. Enter Jesus in the New Testament. He came to earth as a lowly babe, lived a perfect life, and He hung on a cross for sinners like you and I. He did nothing to deserve the ostracizing, torture, and rejection He faced, and yet He went to the cross with a humble willingness that would forever change the trajectory of history and our very lives, should we entrust them to Him.

The Bible is one grand story that tells us of a God who has plans far beyond our wildest dreams. But here's the thing: these dreams are not about us. His dreams are all about His fame and His glory. We just get the privilege of being a part of the incredible story He is weaving together. When we understand the covenant God has given to us, we are able to find a depth of joy that is unparalleled. In Bible times, a covenant was an agreement between two people that could never, ever be broken.

We see one of the most beautiful pictures of a covenant relationship in the Old Testament in the friendship between David and Jonathan. God anointed and chose David as the young, up-and-coming boy king of Israel, and Jonathan was the son of the current king, Saul. These two were friends unlike any other, even though Jonathan's dad grew to absolutely loathe David. Their loyalty to each other was unprecedented and served a foreshadowing of the commitment that God Himself makes to us when He takes us as His own. Let's take a look at part of their story in 1 Samuel 18:

> As soon as he had finished speaking to Saul, the soul of Jonathan was knit to the soul of David, and Jonathan loved him as he loved his own soul. And Saul took him that day and would not let him return to his father's house. Then Jonathan made a covenant with David, because he loved him as his own soul. And Jonathan stripped himself of the robe that was on him and gave it to David, and his armor, and even his sword and his bow and his belt. And David went out and was successful wherever Saul sent him, so that Saul set him over the men of war. And this was good in the sight of all people and also in the sight of Saul's servants. - 1 Samuel 18: 1-5

Jonathan's gestures as the firstborn son of Saul have great significance — Jonathan essentially gave David everything he would need to be Saul's successor. Jonathan gave David his robe, a precious treasure, and also bestowed upon David his own sword, bow, and belt. Jonathan saw to David's every need, ensuring that he would not go without. Jonathan and David were more than the average best friend pair. They were each other's keeper, guardian, and protector. Can you imagine leaving behind your own flesh and blood for someone who was outside of your family? Can you imagine the reactions of your family members if you began to choose someone else above them for the first time ever? These men were each willing to give his life for the other, and they placed the other's needs above his own. Their friendship is an example of the love that can grow between two people who make God the center of their relationship. How often do we see relationships like this? In her Bible study entitled *Covenant: God's Enduring Promises*, Kay Arthur defines the Biblical covenant:

> *Covenant is a solemn, binding agreement...in covenant, two become one...Covenant is seen as a walk into death — death to living for oneself; death to self; death to independent living because you are now in a covenant agreement with another. You have put on each other's robe; you've put on your covenant partner. You've declared that his or her enemies will be your enemies. Your strength will be theirs so that when they are weak they will be strong. If your covenant partner has a need and you have the means of meeting it, you will.*[1]

When you are in a covenant relationship with someone, your life is not your own, because you are bound to that person. Your life takes on their life and vice versa. Their friends are your friends. Their family is your family. Their enemies are your enemies. A covenant relationship is life-altering and dictates how you make decisions and what influences you allow to speak into your thought processes. Within the covenant, you lay down your life and your desires for someone else and they do the same. You are always looking out for them, because a covenant is forever.

So what does all of that have to do with your love life? The fact is this: if you are a follower of Jesus Christ, He has chosen you. You didn't initiate your salvation. You didn't decide to "ask Him into your heart." Hopefully, you said yes to following Him wholeheartedly and allowing His Spirit to completely envelop and transform you.

You have taken on Christ, and He has taken your sin and shame and made you a completely new person because of the blood He shed for you on the cross. And because He has made you new, you are not to live in fear or to live only for the here and now. You are a new creation. As a new creation, you have a new perspective. When things don't go your way, you can praise God for His sovereignty. When you're afraid, you can call on Jesus' name for His strength and might and ask Him to embrace you in His arms. And when you're lonely, you can know that you're never alone.

In this the love of God was made manifest among us, that God sent His only Son into the world so that we might live through Him. In this is love, not that we have loved God but that He loved us and sent His Son to be the propitiation for our sins. - 1 John 4:9-10

We do nothing to initiate the love of God working on our behalf. Everything begins and ends with Him. It is so easy for us to believe that we are in control of our fate, when in reality, it is God who is working behind the scenes, orchestrating a million little details we will never see in order to bring us to each and every situation we count as significant in our lives. And the situations we deem as insignificant? He's using those, too.

When we realize that God's ways truly are higher and better than ours, we can embrace the beauty of His incredible covenant with us. Hebrews 12:2 tells us Jesus is the "founder and perfecter of our faith, who for the joy set before Him endured the cross, despising the shame, and is seated at the right hand of the throne of God." Jesus is seated at the Father's right hand because His work is done. He came to this earth to make us new and to fulfill the promises made by His Father. He came to do the will of His Father, which was to set all things right and make us new. Realizing the beauty of the undeserved covenant love we are in frees us to embrace and fight for hope.

You may be thinking, "How can I have hope when I feel I have been forgotten by God? How can I have hope when I'm the only single friend left in my social circle? How can I have hope when everyone else's life seems to be moving on and mine is at a standstill?" The only way to fight for hope is to receive the love that you have been given by the Father. If you are allowing your marital status, your socioeconomic status, your physical appearance, or your number of followers on social media to define who you are, then you will never walk in the fullness of the covenant of God.

In Exodus 20, we see the dramatic account of how Moses received the Ten Commandments from God on Mount Sinai. These commandments were God's law to the Israelites and His way of communicating to them His expectations for their behavior

90

and standard of living. Here's the thing, though — God knew those commandments were nearly impossible to keep. In order to keep those commandments, the people would need supernatural strength. The pressure of living uprightly all the time would be too much for us if it were up to us. Praise God, it is no longer all on our shoulders, because He has given us His Holy Spirit as our advocate who enables us to love Him with our heart, soul, mind, and strength.

God gave us the new covenant of redemption through His Son, Jesus Christ. Marriage is a beautiful picture of that — the exchange of old for new, the gift of a new name, and the beginning of a new family. But marriage is not the only place we can experience this new covenant. Your relationship with Jesus is the starting point for knowing the covenantal nature of our faithful God. If we come to marriage in hopes that it will fulfill us and change us, we are making an idol out of this earthly, temporal relationship.

The beauty of marriage is that God will use it to sanctify and shape us if we allow Him. But sanctification is not limited to those with a ring on their left finger. This painful, necessary process is for all of us, should we choose to surrender. Hebrews 9:10-13 says,

> *For this is the covenant that I will make with the house of Israel after those days, declares the Lord: I will put my laws into their minds, and write them on their hearts, and I will be their God, and they shall be my people. And they shall not teach, each one his neighbor and each one his brother, saying, 'Know the Lord,' for they shall all know me, from the least of them to the greatest. For I will be merciful toward their iniquities, and I will remember their sins no more.*

How great is our God! We cannot love Him by ourselves. His covenant with us, while beautiful, is so great a burden when we believe it is up to us to perfectly maintain. But praise be to God, who so wonderfully and graciously gives us all things to walk in the light of His grace! We cannot surrender our lives to Him without first feeling His prompting on our hearts. We cannot walk in truth and tear down the lies and strongholds without Him first opening our eyes to the deception. And we cannot be grateful in every season without first understanding that He is always for us.

Our God is a covenant God. He has committed to stand by our side, love us unconditionally, and fight for us in our weakness. And He's never going to let us down or abandon that promise, because that would be against His nature. Friend, He's never going to act against His nature. Ever. It's just not who He is. So no matter where you find yourself today, you can know that if you are in a covenant relationship with Him, the God of the universe is on your side.

If you've never been asked on a date, He sees you.
If you're waiting to have a child, He sees you.
If you're hoping for a job, He sees you.
If you want to change the world for the Gospel but you're shy and timid, He sees you.
If you're tired of living in chronic pain, He sees you.
If you've got big dreams but feel like the underdog, He sees you.

There is nothing we can do to separate ourselves from Him, and He will always, always, always provide exactly what we need, when we need it. That's just who He is. When we find ourselves at a point of desperation and think we are never going to experience a reality different than the one we're living in, He reaches down to remind us that He's still there. He sees us, and He knows. God is a God of constant lovingkindness. Even when we are running away, He pursues us and loves us with extraordinary, undeserved love.

"Can a woman forget her nursing child, that she should have no compassion on the son of her womb? Even these may forget, yet I will not forget you. Behold, I have engraved you on the palms of my hands." - Isaiah 49:15-6a

The temptation we all have is to believe God has forgotten about us or He is uncaring when we do not possess the deepest desires of our hearts. The enemy wants us to believe He is not good, but the truth is God is passionate for His bride. We are His people, and He tethers Himself to us. He cannot forget us because He made us! He created us to know Him, be loved by Him, and be transformed by His unfailing grace. No matter where you are, you must know God is for you and not against you. But how do you stay confident in God's plan when everyone else around you seems to be living your dream life? How do you fight for hope?

The beauty of our relationship with God is that it is not one-sided. He doesn't expect us to "do all the work." No, our God faithfully speaks to us if we will listen, and He reminds us of who He is in the midst of each season. Author Annie Downs says in her memoir *Looking for Lovely*:

> *God gives us permission to feel. There's no demand on your life to bite the bullet and be stronger than the hurt and pain. Yet the directive is the same: rejoice in your sufferings, persevere in them, let your character grow, and watch as hope blooms.*[2]

What we do with our unmet needs and unfulfilled desires is indicative of what we believe about who God is. We must remember that God never changes, and we have to hold onto His promises and saturate our mind with His truth in order to rest in His unchanging grace. His covenantal and unchanging love will only hold us if we allow Him to be God in our lives.

Chapter 13

Understanding Expectations

"We won't be distracted by comparison if we are captivated with purpose." - Bob Goff

Alright, friend. It's time to get real. I have Rory's permission to share this story with you. It's not the cutest or sweetest of stories, but I hope the Lord can use my unfortunate decisions to help you know what not to do.

Unless you fell asleep during the first half of this book, you know that I waited a long time for my husband. Twenty-six years to be exact. And these years were not full of other boyfriends and relationships. Nope, that was not the case my friends. Because Rory? He was boyfriend number one. We aren't counting middle school relationships, so he earned the top spot and will now hold it forever.

As a child, my dreams of marriage and love and relationships were tied up in what I thought was the perfect picture of romance — flowers (every week at least), long walks, romantic dinners, exquisite trips, big diamonds, the whole enchilada. And while I can now say I've been on the receiving end of almost all those things, sometimes my flesh can rear its ugly head in the form of unspoken and unmet expectations that fester into anger and bitterness.

Our first Valentine's Day was the sweetest. Rory knew he was my first valentine, so he wanted to be sure he made it special for me. He bought me roses, planned a day trip, and made reservations at a beautiful restaurant. It was incredible, and I was super impressed and touched with his thoughtfulness. So our first married Valentine's Day rolled around, and I thought it was only going to be exponentially greater because we were married. Duh!

Since Valentine's Day crowds can be obnoxious, we decided to do most of our celebrating on the Friday before. We went to a lovely dinner, and Rory presented me with tickets to the Fox Theatre in Atlanta to see The Sound of Music (I DIED). Poor thing forgot the card at work, though. It's the thought that counts. I was super excited to see The Sound of Music with him, and so touched that he would sacrifice to get us tickets to the show when we were trying to be good with our budget. That Saturday, we went to a beautiful pageant and banquet for a local organization called Extra Special People, so we got dressed up, which was so fun. It was a beautiful event, and we enjoyed the "free" fancy date as a perk from Rory's job at St. Mary's Hospital.

You're probably reading this and thinking, "Jessica, that sounds like such a lovely weekend. You are such a blessed woman to have such a kind and thoughtful husband." Well. First year of marriage Jessica didn't think it was quite enough. Where were the flowers? Where were the big gestures? Where was the surprise? The romance?

Valentine's Day fell on a Sunday during our first year of marriage, and I woke up feeling disappointed with the lack of pizzazz. I mean, I deserved this. I had waited so long to finally have a husband and now he wasn't doing what I wanted him to do. So I sulked and pouted until he finally asked me what was wrong. And when I told him, I crushed his spirits. My ungrateful attitude put a huge damper on the day that was hard to recover from. And when I forced the expectations to become requirements, I sucked all the fun out of the holiday.

Why in the world would I share this with you? Because I believe that God has something to show us when we are confronted with our ugliness. When I threw a temper tantrum on Valentine's Day, who was I reflecting? It certainly wasn't Christ. Was I giving any glory to the Father in those moments? My guess would be a big no.

When I try to control everything by planning out each part of how I will receive and enjoy each holiday, it takes the joy out of it. When my expectations get in the way, I am no longer present or just enjoying the gift that I have in my husband himself. Because he's a pretty amazing gift just as he is. Love can be expressed with flowers and surprises and diamonds. But it's so much more than that. It's shared memories, heartaches, dreams, struggles, victories, and trials.

Whether you're single or married, your calling is to set your mind on things above. The things of this earth are not where we find our ultimate fulfillment. And marriage? It's a thing of this earth. For we who call ourselves followers of Christ are His bride! There is immeasurable joy, satisfaction, and beauty in that alone when we grasp just how amazing He is and begin to long for Him with everything we are.

So when we put our hopes and dreams on one person and expect them to fulfill our happiness, we play a very dangerous game. Jesus is our ultimate source of satisfaction, hope, and joy. And when we decide to place our everything in Him and live in gratitude for the amazingly generous gifts that come from our good Father, our lives are all the more enjoyable. Life is to be enjoyed, after all.

Whether we realize it or not, we all have expectations which influence how we view the world. These expectations, if left unchecked, can be detrimental to our very lives. When we live with our expectations framing our perspective, we often miss out on what is right in front of us. In the past couple years, tracing the root of my expectations so I can better understand my heart and then be changed for the better has been a beneficial practice. I want us to take a look into where exactly those monsters called expectations come from and what to do when they subtly (or not so subtly) creep into our realities.

YOUR UPBRINGING

Every one of us was born into a family not of our choosing, yet we know that God alone placed us in our families on purpose and for a purpose. This fact brings with it various challenges. Your family may have been overly affectionate and encouraging, or it may have been cold and uninviting. You may have a background of a Christ-centered marriage modeled for you, or you may know the pain of abuse, divorce, or neglect. Whatever the case, each one of us has a different paradigm according to what life handed us, and whether we like it or not, this paradigm influences and can even dictate our responses to our spouse's own paradigm.

In our premarital counseling, Rory and I worked through a questionnaire that had over one hundred questions. These questions addressed various issues that will inevitably surface in the context of the marriage relationship — money, time, intimacy, conflict resolution, and more. When we took the time to talk through these issues, I naively thought that because we had discussed them, there would not be much room for conflict. Boy, was I wrong! Even though we had discussed many issues in our premarital counseling, it was only the beginning! These issues are apt to rear their ugly heads whenever and wherever, because we have a very real enemy of our souls who does not like to see happy marriages or healthy homes.

1 Peter 4:12 reminds us of the importance of knowing our true enemy: "Beloved, do not be surprised at the fiery trial when it comes upon you to test you, as though something strange were happening to you." Our enemy is cunning and wants us to believe the worst about our families of origin, our spouse, and our spouses' family. Understanding the importance of sorting through your upbringing cannot be understated. There are big and little ways that your families' traditions, mannerisms, and values shaped you, and you are both bringing something entirely different to the table.

Marriage (and life in general) is not the place to believe that your way is the best way. It is not the place to fight to be right and to have the last word. It is, however, the place and time to consider one another's feelings as you talk through both sides of whatever issue you're facing and come up with a new way — your new family's way — together. And always remember that no matter how good or bad you think you had it growing up, your parents did the best they could with what they had. As an adult, married or single, you can choose to remember the best of times and incorporate those good things into your new life.

Real life example: Rory likes for the dishes to be washed in the dishwasher for sanitary reasons. He's got this thing about how hot the water has to get for all the dishes to be sanitized. Me? I don't mind doing a combination of both dishwasher and hand washing because I like the kitchen to be clean at the end of each night. When we first got married, I was so irked, because I would cook dinner and then ask him to do the dishes. Our house rule growing up was that if you cooked, then others helped clean up. So when Rory would load the dishwasher but then leave the rest of the dishes in the sink, I was so perturbed because I didn't think he was doing what I had asked him to do! When I finally explained my side and he explained his, we were able to reach a middle ground. Was I right? Was he wrong? It's neither. This expectation is tied to upbringing and preference, and I've learned to live with less than perfect because my relationship with my husband is more important than my kitchen being immaculately clean at night. Besides, if it were that important to me, I'd do it myself. And most of the time, it just isn't worth it.

PEERS

Y'all, this one is tough. It is a good thing to look to other married couples to learn from them and glean wisdom. It is not a good thing to look to other married couples and think you have to do exactly what they do. It's just not healthy. We've all seen the "comparison is the thief of joy" quote milling around the internet, and it is true! When we look to others and feel we have to imitate them in order to be successful, we've taken it too far and aren't allowing ourselves to walk in the identity God gave us.

I consider myself a highly sensitive person. It has taken me my whole life to figure this out and begin to embrace it. God made me sensitive, and it's completely okay! Because I am a sensitive person, I can often take on others emotions without even realizing it. Or I can look at someone else's life and feel that in order to be successful, I have to do everything the exact same way she does. This is a self-defeating way to live. There is no way that emulating someone else's life can bring God glory.

"Then I observed that most people are motivated to success because they envy their neighbors. But this too, is meaningless - like chasing the wind." Ecclesiastes 4:4 (NLT)

The writer of Hebrews encourages us to "lay aside every weight, and sin which clings so closely, and let us run with endurance the race that is set before us, looking to Jesus, the founder and perfecter of our faith" (Hebrews 12:1-2) Living with our eyes fixed on Jesus is the only way to succeed. The Scripture does not tell us to run Betty Sue or Suzi Q's race. We are called to run our race. God gave us our one life specifically and intentionally. We must be aware of all God did to bring us to Himself and then allow that to inform our everyday living by making choices which not only honor Him, but are good for our spiritual, mental, and emotional health. I can tell you that making decisions based on what others think or just to keep up with them is not a healthy way to live. We must allow God to love us in the midst of our imperfection so we can rest in Him by owning our story and our life.

In *Comparison Trap: Choosing Contentment in an Age of Awareness*, Sandra Stanley writes: "We can spend lots of time on envy and end up with nothing to show for our efforts."[1]When I compare my personal race to someone else's, I lose every time. I can easily believe I am doing something wrong if I haven't made it to the latest life "checkbox" when my best friend does. When I allow "my" accomplishments and completion of life stages to define me, I've got it all wrong, in marriage and in life. I cannot allow others to define me. And yet I buy into the lie that I'm doing something wrong if my life looks different from my friend's life. I wonder if I'm missing something and grow paranoid thinking about how I could be doing it all wrong.

Real life example: Through talking with friends, I've learned about how other couples manage their finances and thought, "We're doing it ALL WRONG! In order to be successful we have to do the exact same thing as them!" These are LIES! I cannot copy them and then hope for the best. Each decision I make must be guided by the word of God and filtered through honest conversation with my husband.

MOVIES, TV, AND BOOKS

This area of influence is a big soapbox for me, because I believe it is one of the most detrimental ways in which the enemy suckers us women into false ways of thinking, and we in turn are greatly disappointed. As a child, I was a voracious reader. I still love to read, but I just don't have the time I used to have to devour books as I would like to. Movies and television are also a way of escape for me in which I can just relax and enjoy a good story. Hear me when I say I absolutely do not believe movies, television, and books are the devil incarnate. There is nothing inherently evil in these things. However, I think it is imperative for us to realize just how much the stories and thoughts expressed in these media outlets forms our thinking. I remember hearing chick flicks likened to "girl porn" once. While the comparison seems harsh and crass, I believe it is spot on in that romantic comedies and the like warp our thinking. We begin to believe that we deserve the fairy tale and the perfect ending. And friends, life just isn't like that. With the Lord, it is so. much. better. And it is often not tied up neatly in a little bow.

When you are making decisions about what to read or watch, be sure to submit these decisions to the Lord. It may seem "extreme," but I truly believe that we must guard our hearts and minds against wrong ways of thinking and lifestyles that do not align with God's standard. I am by no means perfect at doing this, but I have learned a lot about the importance of protecting my heart and mind. There are so many new television shows and movies today with plots, subplots, and themes so completely unlike God's way that women and men alike intake without a second thought. And what's crazy about the intake of these television shows and movies is that those of us who are Christ followers are laughing at the same crass jokes and rationalizing away the same storylines as our non-believing counterparts. In all honesty, using my discernment to choose what I intake is a real struggle for me. Sometimes I want to be able to talk about the latest show everyone else can't stop gabbing about. I want to be able to get the jokes that are part of everyone's vernacular. But more than that, I want to honor God and protect my heart and mind.

Because I spent so much time escaping into books, movies, and television as a child and teenager, I know the effects this time spent in the weeds has had on my mind. Movies especially can influence our thought processes because we watch real people on the screen and believe our lives could actually somewhat resemble what we see unfold before us in two hours or less. But the truth is, not everything gets wrapped up easily, and the guy does not always have a cute one-liner to offer when he messes up. The truth is that life is really messy and complicated and sometimes you hurt the ones you love the most and you don't apologize right away and then kiss and make up.

Real life example: See Valentine's Day story above. :)

SOCIAL MEDIA

We have media where the stories are obviously not real and written by paid Hollywood screenwriters and acted out in front of us by gorgeous celebrities, and then we have social media. We can scroll through Facebook, Twitter, or Instagram and see friends with whom we attended college or youth group and wonder how their lives seem to be so perfectly curated all. the. dang. time. But we forget this one simple fact: social media is a highlight reel. When I was teaching elementary school, I often had people tell me how adorable the videos of my kids were that I posted during our "brain break" dance times. What they didn't see is how I "raised my voice" (read: yelled) at a kid minutes before for his disobedience. Social media is an incredible outlet, but it still does not give us the whole story.

Social media is not of the devil, either. The various social media outlets we have at our fingertips can be used for God's glory as well. There are literally millions of users on Facebook, Twitter, and Instagram, and when we post there or go there to scroll through our feeds, we can get a glimpse of what's going on in the lives of others around us. And while that can be disheartening or maddening, it can also be encouraging. When we decide to follow others who are on a mission to set the world on fire for Jesus, we can be inspired to do the same. While we cannot know the intimate details of the lives of hundreds of people on each social media platform, watching them from afar can actually be a sort of mentorship if we allow others who truly know Christ to influence us and fill our feeds.

My sweet friend Gretchen of Well-Watered Women Co. has a beautifully inspirational Instagram feed with literally thousands of followers. But instead of using that platform to showcase the put together and tidied parts of her life, she leverages this platform to share her struggles - little and not-so-little. The images are often beautiful, but her captions are like mini-blog posts in which she bares her soul and shares her heart. She encourages women every day to walk in the light of the truth and to use their influence to love others and share the light of Christ. We have talked several times about the beauty and the difficulty of social media, and she wrote the following on her blog:

> *If I leave this online mission field because I'm tired of fighting the fight of the faith, I've let the enemy have victory. The enemy is having a field day stealing women's identities, precious time, and purpose through the internet. He is celebrating each time we pull up our feeds and compare ourselves to other women while grumbling against what God has given us. He knows that if he can distract God's people from our greater calling that he has won a small victory. But we serve a God who has won the entire battle, and people need to hear this message.*[1]

If we say we are believers of Jesus, every single bit of our lives better reflect that. He does not call us to perfection, but He does ask us to walk in a manner worthy of the calling of Christ. Knowing when to take a step back from social media can not only protect our hearts and minds, but will also protect our relationships as we seek to live in the now instead of on our screens.

Real life example: My friend posts a picture of her awesome date night, and my heart twinges with jealousy. "Why don't we do things like that? They're so cool." How do I even know what they were really doing that night? If I had married 30 years ago, I most likely would have no idea what they were doing with their Friday night, and it would not have made a difference to me. Let's chase contentment and leave comparison behind. Our lives are too short to get lost in the world of jealousy when God has given us so much to steward and be grateful for.

Let's pause and think about where our expectations come from and how to make a mental shift. It takes time to unpack our expectations and to truly allow the Lord to renew the mind. But when we allow Him to show us the evidences of His grace, we can slowly begin to be grateful for every little thing and outsmart the monster in our minds. Don't allow your expectations to get in the way of your reality. Your heart and mind will thank you later.

Chapter 14

Transformed by Love

And I am sure of this, that he who began a good work in you will bring it to completion at the day of Jesus Christ. - Philippians 1:6

Sorting through the various emotions evoked at the beginning of our marriage was a process. Honestly, it is a journey I am still on ¬— one of understanding where my true worth and value lie. When I began to liken Rory's love for me to God's love for me, I was so moved. I asked the Lord why He saw fit to give me Rory, and He told me, plain as day, "To show you how much I love you." You see, as an older child, it is easy for me to walk in the characteristics of my stereotype and worldly labels —perfectionist, type A, controlling, bossy, etc. And while those things are true about me when I'm at my worst, those characteristics are not the ones that God Himself chooses to see when He looks at me. Because of my desire to be perfect and the impossibility of attaining this perfection, I thought I was too worthless to be loved. I never would have said it aloud, but I believed that no one would love me if they knew "the real truth" about my seasons of running fast and hard away from Perfect Love.

Maybe you feel the same way, friend. Have you ever wondered if you are worthy of love? Not just love from a significant other or potential spouse, but love from God Himself? Have you ever thought you just aren't good enough and something is wrong with you? Have you fixed your eyes on your circumstances and determined them to be unchangeable and immovable? I know I have thought all of the above was true and then some. It is easy to believe the promises of God are true for everyone but you and begin to walk in a victim mentality. You can begin to believe that maybe He just doesn't actually mean what He says. This victim mentality can translate into all sorts of seasons and circumstances. God's word says in John 8 that "you will know the truth, and the truth will set you free." Knowing the truth of who God is transforms our very lives.

Now, I know God's love is not like our love. Our love is fickle and changing. We decide we love someone based on what they can do for us and how they can satisfy our needs, desires, and wishes. But His love is pure and kind. It is steadfast and strong. It never wavers and never falters. His love cannot be quantified or changed. It is immovable and fierce. His love pursues — even to the deepest depths when you think you've gone too far. His love never ever ever gives up.

All my life, I thought I had to work to make God love me. I knew all the right Bible verses and could tell you I was saved by grace through faith, but I didn't really believe it. I figured it was too good to be true. It turns out it is so good and true. All the time I spent beating myself up over things I couldn't control and decisions that I couldn't take back, it hurt the heart of my Father, who sent His Son to the cross so I could be found by Him, know Him, and be known by Him. Just as Boaz redeemed Ruth, I was finding that Rory was my very own Boaz, leading and guiding me to truth and helping to heal the innermost places that had been covered up for so long.

Being loved like this is overwhelming at times, because it doesn't seem real or fair. Sometimes I still have to pinch myself and question if this man that God gave me is actually real. But then I roll over and he's right there, morning after morning. I cannot tell you how much this love means to me. And the beautiful thing about this love is it's but a mere shadow of the love of the Father.

So we have come to know and to believe the love that God has for us. God is love, and whoever abides in love abides in God, and God abides in him...There is no fear in love, but perfect love casts out fear. For fear has to do with punishment, and whoever fears has not been perfected in love. We love because he first loved us. If anyone says, "I love God," and hates his brother, he is a liar, for he who does not love his brother whom he has seen cannot love God whom he has not seen. And this commandment we have from him: whoever loves God must also love his brother. - 1 John 4:16,18-21

When we believe the God of the universe chose us and redeemed us, we won't spend our time trying to win the love of others or hoping that their affirmations will keep us afloat. Knowing the love of God is the most precious gift we can choose to receive. His love is what sustains us and carries us when others fail us. Yes, the love of my husband is incredibly life-giving. Yes, he encourages me to remember the truth of who God is and who God says I am. But at the end of the day, he is not God.

One of my sweet mentors said to me once, "You're married, and you love your husband, but he's not enough. You're still caught up in waiting for your fairy tale, and Jesus is the real fairy tale. He's not too good to be true. He's real and loves you." I cannot allow my love for Rory to supersede my love for God, nor can he do the same with his love for me. We cannot put each other on pedestals and hang all of our hopes and dreams on each other. When I was single, I thought that when my Prince Charming came, he would rescue me from all the hurt and pain I had kept locked away for so long. This hurt and pain was from various life circumstances common to many of us, and I had not fully processed and dealt with it in a healthy way. It turns out my Prince Charming, while handsome and sweet as the day is long, can only do so much. And honestly, having him actually complicates things and can make life harder, because all my junk is exposed. But that's where the true life is found. Fighting through the brokenness is how we've become closer and how God's love has shone in, through, and around us. We spend so much time trying to cover up our brokenness or sweep it under the rug. But God wants to take our brokenness and make us new. He wants to make us gold.

In *Chasing Slow*, Erin Loechner writes:

My friend Mai once told me about kintsugi, a Japanese tradition in which broken pottery is repaired with a metallic-infused lacquer. Kintsugi means "to patch with gold;" in this technique, the potter mends a bowl in delicate, sweeping strokes, taking no care to hide the crack. There are no clear coats, there is no blending, there is no attempt at concealing what has occurred. Instead, the crack is illuminated with gold, with respect, with observance.

And then it is pieced together — not to be made new but to be changed.
The break itself is the beauty.
The crack is worthy of gold.
Can you imagine it?
Kintsugi celebrates failure in a way I am still learning to do, in a way I am only beginning to understand…

I once asked my friend what the secret to kintsugi is. Is it the brush? The application? The adhesive, the gold?

"Nah," she said. "It's just time. When my uncle does it, it can take, like, two months."[1]

Time. Something that often is not friendly nor fun. And yet time, prayer, and a whisper (or a few shouts) from God Himself are what He uses to bring us His healing in His way. And I wouldn't trade this for anything. How often have I despised the process of being made into gold? How many times have I resisted the work of the Holy Spirit in my life by desperately clinging to the old ways which only bring my demise? How many times have I missed out on God's best for me because I was concerned with my agenda?

God is not looking to make us into better versions of ourselves. He's looking to make us into the image of His Son. And friends, that takes time. Whether you are old or young, married or single, God is not finished with you yet, and His transforming work is for you. His love is for you. His heart is for you, and He longs to cover you with His wings and help you know His fierce and abiding love.

When we resist the work of God in our lives, we resist the beauty of His grace and mercy as evidence to a watching world. When we neglect to allow God to change us and make us new, we are saying that our ways are better and deceiving ourselves to believe we are somehow in control. Beth Moore explains the law of the harvest and the seasons in her teaching on the book of James. She shares how we must understand the law of the harvest and the meaning of the seasons by accepting the beauty of the process. She also issues the challenge to actively acknowledge His faithfulness, stating that sometimes "we want a Holy Spurt instead of a Holy Spirit."[2]

We do not like the process, friends. We want a quick fix more than we want to experience Jesus. We often despise the story God has placed us in because we are too busy looking to the right or to the left, or allowing our past or worries of the future to bog us down. We read stories of valiant men and women who God used for His kingdom — they shut the mouths of lions, defied Nazi rule, marched in demonstrations against hatred, and overcame unthinkable odds in the name of Jesus. We say we want to live lives of unwavering trust in our Savior, but do we want to do what it takes to get there? Later in the teaching, Beth encourages listeners with this simple question — "Do you want a good story or not?"

My natural desire is to hope for a life of ease and comfort. I want everything to go as planned and I want to live life on my terms. But following Christ is the exact opposite of ease and comfort. Following Christ means you lay down your life for His sake, because you have been transformed by His amazing love. When we truly see Jesus for Who He is, in His beauty and majesty, covered in grace, we cannot stay the same.

He had no form or majesty that we should look at him, and no beauty that we should desire him. He was despised and rejected by men; a man of sorrows, and acquainted with grief; and as one from whom men hide their faces he was despised, and we esteemed him not. Surely he has borne our griefs and carried our sorrows; yet we esteemed him stricken, smitten by God, and afflicted. But he was pierced for our transgressions; he was crushed for our iniquities; upon him was the chastisement that brought us peace, and with his wounds we are healed. - Isaiah 53:2b-5

Jesus went to the cross to fulfill the will of the Father. The will of the Father was to restore all things to Himself. When Adam and Eve sinned in the Garden, everything changed. When we begin to realize the depths of the wounds we carry because of our past — what we've done or what has been done to us — it can feel like too much. The pain of changing and working through our sin and our scars is sometimes unbearable. But Jesus bore our sin and shame on the cross. He took on death so we may experience life, and when we allow His unfailing love to change our hearts and minds, nothing will ever be the same.

There is no emotion or heartache we can experience that is unfamiliar to King Jesus. And because He truly knows our pain, He can enter into our suffering and our struggles with us. He intercedes for us and allows His Holy Spirit to act as our great comforter when we feel like we are too far gone. Romans 8 tells us there is absolutely nothing that can separate us from our God. Singleness cannot separate us from God. Loneliness cannot separate us from God. Our past cannot separate us from God. The powers of hell itself cannot separate us from God. And yet we spend our time wondering if His love for us is true and unfailing.

If I spent all of my time wondering if Rory really loved me, we would have some serious issues to work through. Yet I do this very thing in my relationship with God when I choose to operate from striving and hustling for my worth instead of walking in the love and grace He has so lavishly poured upon me. Understanding His love for me changes everything. Everything.

My definition and understanding of love has grown in the last couple years. Walking beside Rory as his wife is my greatest privilege and honor. Being loved by him truly is the greatest gift. On our first wedding anniversary, I wrote the following on my blog:

What Love Is
Love is when you take out the trash when you really would rather sit on the couch.
Love is being a shoulder to cry on and a hand to hold onto.
Love is when Ror makes dinner because I'm an emotional mess and just can't even.
Love is watching a movie you'd rather sleep through — and staying awake.

Love is driving during a road trip when you're tired, too.
Love is being excited when your best friend comes home from
work.
Love is loading and unloading the dishwasher.
Love is making brownies just because.
Love is a card on your dashboard to wish you a good day.
Love is choosing to let it go instead of fighting to have the last
word and be heard.
Love is getting dressed up for a date night and getting the
appetizers and drinks, too.
Love is silly nicknames that are super lame and mushy
because they're just more fun that way.
Love is early morning cuddle sessions.
Love is late night prayers after a bad dream.
Love is tolerating hangry diatribes.
Love is breakfast in bed.
Love is Netflix and chill (in a fort, of course) for date night.
Love is a look across the room that needs no words.
Love is laughing until you cry and can't breathe because your
stomach hurts so bad.
Love is way too much fun.
Love is being known in all the best and worst ways.
Love is hard.
Love is good.
Love is worth it.

God has used the context of marriage to show me Himself in ways that He did not during my singleness. That does not mean that I am an "enlightened" or "special" person — it is just God being God and using my season to teach me. When I see my sin in front of my face for what feels like the millionth time (that day), I can become discouraged. I wonder why I make the same mistakes over and over and why I can't seem to "get it together." But God is not sitting in heaven shaking His head and wondering when I'm going to finally straighten up. He sees all of me, and He loves me anyway. And because I know His great love, I can walk in freedom by allowing His love to change every bit of me into a beautiful reflection of His amazing grace.

Chapter 15

What to Do with a Waiting Heart

Rejoice always, pray without ceasing, give thanks in all circumstances; for this is the will of God in Christ Jesus for you. - 1 Thessalonians 5:16-18

Let's face it. We are all waiting for something. Maybe you're waiting to graduate, get married, have a baby, buy a house, get a job...the possibilities are endless. Maybe you're literally waiting in line as you read this book. We all know the agony of waiting for something we long for and want so badly it hurts. But what do we do when that thing doesn't come when or how we want it? What if we've been waiting on it for a long time and there seems to be no hope on the horizon? How do we know when it's time to move on from a dream?

Hope deferred makes the heart sick, but a desire fulfilled is a tree of life. - Proverbs 13:12

In middle school, I couldn't wait to be in high school. In high school, I couldn't wait to drive and go to college. In college, I couldn't wait to have a boyfriend. In my early twenties, I still couldn't wait to have a boyfriend. When I *finally* got a boyfriend, I couldn't wait to get married. Now that we're married, I can't wait to have a baby. When does it stop?

Comparison isn't just the thief of joy, it's the thief of everything. Keep your eyes on your purposeful path. Celebrate others... Cultivate gratitude over comparison. Gratitude turns what we have into more than enough. - Lara Casey[1]

You know what they say. The grass is always greener on the other side, but someone's got to mow it. Here's what I've learned and what I know to be true: coveting and comparison are a certain death to the heart. There is no joy in wanting your neighbor's story, house, car, job, wardrobe, etc. There is no life in wishing away your day and daydreaming about the "someday" when your life will be made new and your dreams will come true. There is no hope found in placing your entire worth in nominal things. None.

I have spent so much time longing and pining for the next season in pretty much every season of my life. Where is the joy in that? There isn't any. There can't be any. Because God didn't give us today for the next season or for tomorrow. He gave us today for today's sake. It's a gift to be cherished and there is amazing work being done in, through, and around us, if we look up to see it.

It is so very easy to look around in whatever stage you find yourself and feel as though you are being left behind. I've been there, and I really do get it. I got my license a few months (maybe it was weeks, but to a 16-year-old it felt like years) late. I didn't kiss a boy until I was twenty-six. I was in six weddings before I was the bride. I. get. it.

When we compare our story to our friend's story, we are saying to God that what He has given us just isn't quite enough; it doesn't quite fit the ticket. And that's not aligning our hearts with truth. It's not walking in confidence of His promises. And it's certainly not living surrendered.

There is a dangerous zone to desires of the heart that we enter into when they begin to consume us. The desires we have for marriage, children, and the like are God-given desires, and there is innately nothing wrong with them. Proverbs 30:15b-16 says,

> *Three things are never satisfied;*
> *four never say, "Enough":*
> *Sheol, the barren womb,*
> *the land never satisfied with water,*
> *and the fire that never says, "Enough."*

If we allow our desires to consume us, we will never be satisfied. When our desire becomes a demand, it is much like a poison, seeping into every area of our lives and tainting it for the worse. In seasons of deep grief, sorrow, and disappointment, my desires which became demands tainted my relationships with

112

others, my view of God, and my mental and emotional stability. We cannot allow the enemy to have victory in this way. We must, we must, we must allow the Spirit of God to transform our hearts and minds as we cling to Him as our only hope.

There have been seasons in my life where my waiting heart was so frustrated that I allowed my desires to completely burn up my entire life. I was jealous of friends, making up stories about their lives and how much better theirs were than mine. I was frustrated with God, falsely believing I had to prove myself to Him to manipulate His hand and get Him to give me what I believed I deserved. This is a scary place to be. And yet I have found myself there when I neglect to remind myself of His promises and rehearse the truth of His character each day.

When we are suffering from deep disappointment and feelings of isolation, we have to cling to what we know to be true. We must preach the Gospel to ourselves day in and day out. Walking in the truth is not easy, but it is worth it. For our friendships, our families, and our health, it is so worth it.

On July 23, 2014, I wrote the following in my journal:

> *Lord, help me not to be afraid to pray big things. I am so very grateful for the life You have given me. I love my family and friends. You have given me my dream job. You have shown me my purpose here on earth in Athens, but also in Africa! You are constantly showing me more of Yourself and helping me to see Your heart. You are constantly giving me new dreams to dream with You and asking me to do things I've never done before. And I'm learning that You are there in the unknown and the uncertainty. You are always there. You fill me with Your Spirit and show me just how awesome You are. Your grace is sufficient for me. Your love is enough for me. Your joy is unspeakable and wells up inside of me. And I want to walk with You all the days of my life.*

> *Lord, as grateful as I am for my life, I still have a yearning desire in my heart for a husband. You have given me that desire, and You have also told me that it would be fulfilled. Would You help me to be patient as I*

continue to wait on You? I know that You are still working behind the scenes in ways that I can't see.

Lord, those are my dreams and desires. Once again, I lay them at Your feet. I ask that you protect my future husband from the evil one. Would You help him stand firm when faced with hard decisions that could compromise his integrity? Would You show him how much you love him and help him to find his confidence in You?

Lord, I have dealt with so many insecure and trifling men. My patience is wearing thin. I ask that my future husband be bold. You told me a year ago that all You wanted me to do was wait, trust, and pray. Well, Lord, I pray that my future husband seeks Your face before approaching me and that he gets a clear word from You. I pray that You fill his heart with peace and that You open his eyes at just the right time. I ask that You calm my anxious heart and help me to just enjoy each season — dating, engagement, and then marriage as it should be enjoyed. Help me to fix my eyes on You so that I look to You as my all in all and not to him.

I ask that You give me a deeper love for You each day and that my love for You is always the source of my love for him. May he never be my god. I want to love You with all that I am, even though I know that You will also give me a love for him. May Your love be the foundation of our relationship, and may Your kingdom be advanced as a result of our union.

There's no way I could have known that one year later, I would have a new name. I had no idea that my future husband was moving to Athens and finding his place. I had no idea that he would begin visiting my church and he would begin putting down roots in my beloved Classic City. I had no idea. But God. God knew. God saw. And God orchestrated every single detail and brought us together at just the right time for His glory and our good. And I would not change a thing.

Here's my hope. My hope is that we live lives of gratitude and complete surrender, knowing we can run our race and say thank you every step of the way. Because He is right there with us and He has amazing plans for us beyond our wildest dreams. It just means we need to get out of the way. And I don't know about you, but I could stand to get out of the way more often than I'd like to admit. May we rest in His grace and know His embrace.

So what do you do with your waiting heart? You give it to Jesus. You ask for more grace. You understand that there is so much joy to be found in the here and now. You beg for even more grace. And you bathe your heart and mind in His truth, asking for a greater outpouring of His Spirit in your heart and life in order to love others as He so mercifully loves you.

Conclusion

In these pages, I share my story not solely to give you something entertaining to read, but to point you to the one true God. Only He can move and orchestrate things in His perfect timing. Every single thing I have gone through in my life — sins and secrets, loneliness, and frustration with long-forgotten dreams — has been worth it. Because every single circumstance has pointed me to Him. He is so worthy of my praise. He is my redeemer, savior, friend and confidant. My life's purpose is to know Him and to make Him known. I exist to fall more madly in love with Him with each passing day, and in turn to point others to Him by allowing them to see just how good He is through my life. I'm not perfect or worth any accolades. But He is. And that's what I hope you see as a result of reading through this account of what He's done for me, because it's His story.

It's interesting how instrumental God's timing can be. When I started writing this book, my husband and I had been trying to conceive a child for about a month. As I continued to work on this book and dig deeper into its message, month after month went by. One day after reading a draft of the book, my husband gently reminded me of some things I had written. He said, "You know, this sounds kind of familiar. In your book, you talked about how you were so busy wishing for marriage that you missed out on other things. And now you are so obsessed with getting pregnant — do you see any themes?" Man did that one hurt. He was so right, and he was echoing exactly what the Holy Spirit had already been telling me the same thing in my time with Him as I worked on this book. I finally told Him, "Lord, please let this be the last time I learn this lesson. It's too hard to keep going through it again!" And you know what? The Lord has done so much in my heart since then. Every day is not easy or perfect, but His sustaining grace strengthens me and helps me to take each day as it comes, ready to walk with Him. My prayer is that you understand that no matter what you're waiting for and pining for and daydreaming about, God has you in His hands, and He has surely not forgotten about you.

When I dreamed about being married as a little girl, I often envisioned flowers, romantic dinners, and a perfect little home. We're only a few years into this, and already my perspective on what love is has changed so much. The love we had for each other in the beginning was so bright-eyed and fun, and now I feel that our love is so much deeper. The last year brought with a deep heartache and sorrow — infertility does that to a person. But God. God is so much greater than anything we come against — be it loneliness, rejection, or heartbreak. And He has used my husband to teach me of His steadfast love and unchanging grace. I can only imagine how I will feel when we are 20 years in with kids and so much more history between us and a family that we call our own. I still stand by my thoughts that I wrote just a few months into our first year — marriage isn't hard. Life is hard. But marriage is good. And life is good when we allow God to be our everything.

Bonus

Real Talk with My Husband

When and how did you come to know the Lord and begin to follow Him?

I came to know the Lord at a young age, a similar story to most who grew up in the church. I have had many good seasons and many complacent seasons in my walk with the Lord, but have always been blessed to have many good friends and mentors investing in me along the way.

How do you think the Lord allows you to give Him glory in your job?

I think the main thing we can do to give glory to God is to do our jobs well. I think being excellent at what you do is a great way to give God glory, especially if you are remembering to rely on Him in all things! I think another big factor that can give God glory is the kind of atmosphere you create. Does the attitude in the room change when you are in the room (for better or worse)? Do people enjoy being around you? How do you handle disagreements and conflict? Do you stress others out with your stress? I think how we handle ourselves in a work environment can show people how Jesus has transformed us.

What have you learned about yourself and the Lord through marriage?

I have definitely learned about taking life day by day. When you begin to just coast through the weeks, it is easy to become complacent in everything. I am learning marriage takes focus and effort each day in order to be a good spouse. Marriage has been a great blessing, because it is a tiny glimpse of our relationship with Jesus. It provides tangible examples of how I should be relating and investing in God and how he is responding to me. For example, when things are hard or frustrating at work, it is easy for me to look past it because I know in a few short hours I will get to see my wife. But in a greater scope of things, that can remind me that Christ is always with me and I can take joy in that now. Little ways that Jess shows me love always point me towards Christ and little ways I show Jess love can ultimately make me more like Christ.

What advice would you give to men still waiting to find a wife?

Sign up for online dating and ask out the first girl who sends you a wink. :) In all seriousness, I don't have any good dating advice, because I was never very good at dating. As I got older though, even just in being friends with females, it became easier and easier for me to identify what I was and was not looking for. I could see personality types that although were enjoyable in friendship were probably not ideal for marriage. Obviously, differences are good in marriage, but there are certain things you should never compromise on. The longer you are single, the easier it becomes to look past red flags. You can easily get desperate and excuse red flags that you should not excuse.

What advice would you give to women still waiting on a husband?

I would say the best advice I could give women would be to learn how to be content where you are. It is very easy to fall into a trap of thinking that once you find someone and are married, you will be fully happy and all of your problems will melt away. That is not the case, and my wife can confirm that I am not even close to awesome enough to make her happy and solve all of her problems. Learn how to be whole without a spouse, and when you find a husband who is whole without you, it will be a great and freeing relationship. It takes a lot of pressure off of the other person to try and make you happy. If you are not happy where you are now, you are not going to be happy when you are married.

Describe your perfect day.

I love Saturdays with the wife. I think the perfect day starts with sleeping in (not too late) but at least have nothing scheduled that makes you get out of bed. Next would be brunch, eating in or eating out, no preference. If the weather is nice, I'd like to be outside for some of the day. This could include taking our dog Bailey to the park or going to some arts and crafts fair downtown. After a nice relaxing afternoon, there is not much better than a movie on the couch with cheap Chinese or pizza and popcorn.

And last but not least: coffee or tea?

Tea — coffee smells great but leaves a bad aftertaste that no amount of gum can get rid of. Tea is clean and wholesome.

Acknowledgements

It takes a village to write a book. There is absolutely no way I could have done any of this on my own. There are so many people who played a role in making this book come to my life, and I am grateful for each and every one of them.

Rory: my best friend, my confidante, my biggest cheerleader, shoulder to cry on, and the one who just makes everything better. Thank you so much for always encouraging me to do whatever the Lord lays on my heart, even when it sounds crazy. Thank you for the way you listen to Him and show me how to slow down and learn from Him. Thank you for supporting my dreams and for allowing me to share our story. I love you always and always.

My parents: thank you for buying me journals while I was growing up and for letting me process through writing. Thank you for encouraging me to hone my skills and for reading my work!

My sweet in-laws: thank you for letting me become a Mathisen!

Teresa, Kaí, Ms. Suzanne, Melissa, Hannah I., and Hannah H., thank you so much for reading the first and very rough draft and telling me to keep going.

Melissa, thank you so much for all of the wonderful edits you made not only to the grammar, but also to the style of this book. You helped me dig deeper and say things the way they needed to be said! Your insights were invaluable.

Shelby, thank you for all of your patience and kindness with me through the design process. Your creation for the cover is/ was beyond my wildest dreams, and I cannot even believe how much you did to make this book look incredible. Your edits earlier in the game were huge, too. I am incredibly grateful for the way the Lord led me to you and am so in awe of your talent and giftings.

Tori, Amy A., Brooke, and Natalie, thank you for responding to my Facebook inquiry for insight about relationships! I was so glad to include your wisdom in this book.

My wonderful and faithful blog readers, thank you for encouraging me to keep going and for reaching out when the Lord used any of the words He gave me to minister to you!

To my sweet interns and college girls who I have had the privilege of getting to know through the years, this book is for you. I am so honored to get to be a part of your lives and pray that the Lord uses this book to encourage you. I love you so much!

To my sweet Heavenly Father, thank You so much for telling me to write this book. Thank You for divine inspiration and for the way You wrote my story. I wouldn't change a thing, and I am so grateful that You are the Author and not me.

Scripture

Chapter 2

Hope deferred makes the heart sick, but a desire fulfilled is a tree of life. - Proverbs 13:12

Chapter 3

There is a way that seems right to a man, but its end is the way to death. - Proverbs 16:25

Keep your heart with all vigilance, for from it flow the springs of life. – Proverbs 4:23

Be careful what you think, because your thoughts run your life. (NCV) - Proverbs 4:23

Chapter 4

Those who plant in tears will harvest with shouts of joy. They weep as they go to plant their seed, but they sing as they return with the harvest. - Psalm 126:5-6 (NLT)

Do not urge me to leave you or to return from following you. For where you go I will go, and where you lodge I will lodge. Your people shall be my people, and your God my God. Where you die I will die, and there will I be buried. May the Lord do so to me and more also if anything but death parts me from you. - Ruth 1:16-17

Chapter 5

Do not be anxious about anything, but in everything by prayer and supplication with thanksgiving, let your requests be made known to God. And the peace of God, which surpasses all understanding, will guard your hearts and minds in Christ Jesus. - Philippians 4:6-7

Finally, be strong in the Lord and in the strength of his might. Put on the whole armor of God, that you may be able to stand against the schemes of the devil. For we do not wrestle against flesh and blood, but against the rulers, against the authorities, against the cosmic powers over this present darkness, against the spiritual forces of evil in the heavenly places. Therefore, take up the whole armor of God, that you may be able to withstand in the evil day, and having done all, to stand firm. Stand therefore, having fastened on the belt of truth, and having put on the breastplate of righteousness, and, as shoes for your feet, having put on the readiness given by the gospel of peace. In all circumstances take up the shield of faith, with which you can extinguish all the flaming darts of the evil one; and take the helmet of salvation, and the sword of the Spirit, which is the word of God, praying at all times in the Spirit, with all prayer and supplication. - Ephesians 6:10-18

Our soul waits for the Lord; He is our help and our shield. For our heart is glad in Him, because we trust in His holy name. Let your steadfast love, O Lord, be upon us, even as we hope in you. - Psalm 33:20-22

I sought the Lord, and He answered me and delivered me from all my fears. Those who look to Him are radiant, and their faces shall never be ashamed... The Lord is near to the brokenhearted and saves the crushed in spirit." - Psalm 34:4-5, 18

Our soul waits for the Lord; He is our help and our shield. For our heart is glad in Him, because we trust in His holy name. Let your steadfast love, O Lord, be upon us, even as we hope in you. - Psalm 33:20-22

I sought the Lord, and He answered me and delivered me from all my fears. Those who look to Him are radiant, and their faces shall never be ashamed... The Lord is near to the brokenhearted and saves the crushed in spirit. - Psalm 34:4-5, 18

Chapter 6

His thoughts for us outnumber the grains of sand. - Psalm 139:17-18

Hear, O Israel: The Lord our God, the Lord is one. You shall love the Lord your God with all your heart and with all your soul and with all your might. And these words that I command you today shall be on your heart. You shall teach them diligently to your children, and shall talk of them when you sit in your house, and when you walk by the way, and when you lie down, and when you rise. You shall bind them as a sign on your hand, and they shall be as frontlets between your eyes. You shall write them on the doorposts of your house and on your gates. - Deuteronomy 6:4-9

Chapter 7

For we are His workmanship, created in Christ Jesus for good works; which God has prepared beforehand, that we should walk in them. - Ephesians 2:10

Do not be deceived, my beloved brothers. Every good and every perfect gift is from above, coming down from the Father of lights with whom there is no variation or shadow due to change. - James 1:16-17

He who calls you is faithful; He will surely do it.

- 1 Thessalonians 5:24

Know therefore that the Lord your God is God, the faithful God who keeps covenant and steadfast love with those who love him and keep his commandments, to a thousand generations.

- Deuteronomy 7:9

All the paths of the Lord are steadfast love and faithfulness, for those who keep his covenant and his testimonies. - Psalm 25:10

For the word of the Lord is upright, and all his work is done in faithfulness. - Psalm 33:4

For the Lord God is a sun and shield; the Lord bestows favor and honor. No good thing does he withhold from those who walk uprightly. - Psalm 84:11

The steadfast love of the Lord never ceases; his mercies never come to an end; they are new every morning; great is your faithfulness. "The Lord is my portion," says my soul, "therefore I will hope in him."- Lamentations 3:22-24

O Lord, you are my God; I will exalt you; I will praise your name, for you have done wonderful things, plans formed of old, faithful and sure. - Isaiah 25:1

For all the promises of God find their Yes in him. That is why it is through him that we utter our Amen to God for his glory. - 2 Corinthians 1:20

O Lord, you have searched me and known me! You know when I sit down and when I rise up; you discern my thoughts from afar. - Psalm 139:1

We have this as a sure and steadfast anchor of the soul, a hope that enters into the inner place behind the curtain. -Hebrews 6:19

In this world, you will have tribulation. But take heart, I have overcome the world. - John 16:33

The thief comes only to steal and kill and destroy. I came that they may have life and have it abundantly. - John 10:1

Now to Him who is able to do far more abundantly than all that we ask or think, according to the power at work within us, to Him be glory in the church and in Christ Jesus throughout all generations. - Ephesians 3:20-21

Put to death, therefore what is earthly in you: sexual immorality, impurity, passion, evil desire, and covetousness, which is idolatry. - Colossians 3:5

Rejoice always, pray continually, give thanks in all circumstances. - 1 Thessalonians 5:16-18

Chapter 9

Because he bends down to listen, I will pray as long as I have breath! -Psalm 116:2 (NLT)

Chapter 10

I lift up my eyes to the hills.

From where does my help come?

My help comes from the Lord,

who made heaven and earth.

- Psalm 121:1

Now to him who is able to do immeasurably more than all we ask or imagine, according to his power that is at work within us, to him be glory in the church and in Christ Jesus throughout all generations, for ever and ever! Amen. - Ephesians 3:20-21 (NIV)

For those who live according to the flesh set their minds on the things of the flesh, but those who live according to the Spirit set their minds on the things of the Spirit. For to set the mind of the flesh is death, but to set the mind on the Spirit is life and peace. For the mind that is set on the flesh is hostile to God, for it does not submit to God's law; indeed, it cannot. Those are in the flesh cannot please God. - Romans 8:5-8

Be watchful, stand firm in the faith, act like men, be strong. Let all that you do be done in love.

-1 Corinthians 16:13-14

Chapter 11

Give thanks to the Lord, for He is good, for His steadfast love endures forever. - Psalm 136:1

Chapter 12

In this the love of God was made manifest among us, that God sent only Son into the world so that we might live through Him. In this is love, not that we have loved God but that He loved us and sent His Son to be the propitiation for our sins. - 1 John 4:9-10

Looking to Jesus, the founder and perfecter of our faith, who for the joy that was set before him endured the cross, despising the shame, and is seated at the right hand of the throne of God. - Hebrews 12:2

For this is the covenant that I will make with the house of Israel after those days, declares the Lord: I will put my laws into their minds, and write them on their hearts, and I will be their God, and they shall be my people. And they shall not teach, each one his neighbor and each one his brother, saying, 'Know the Lord,' for they shall all know me, from the least of them to the greatest. For I will be merciful toward their iniquities, and I will remember their sins no more. - Hebrews 9:10-13

"Can a woman forget her nursing child, that she should have no compassion on the son of her womb? Even these may forget, yet I will not forget you. Behold, I have engraved you on the palms of my hands." - Isaiah 49:15-6a

Chapter 13

"Beloved, do not be surprised at the fiery trial when it comes upon you to test you, as though something strange were happening to you." - 1 Peter 4:12

Then I observed that most people are motivated to success because they envy their neighbors. But this too, is meaningless - like chasing the wind. - Ecclesiastes 4:4 (NLT)

Let us also lay aside every weight, and sin which clings so closely, and let us run with endurance the race that is set before us, looking to Jesus, the founder and perfecter of our faith. -Hebrews 12:1-2

Chapter 14

And I am sure of this, that he who began a good work in you will bring it to completion at the day of Jesus Christ. - Philippians 1:6

So we have come to know and to believe the love that God has for us. God is love, and whoever abides in love abides in God, and God abides in him...There is no fear in love, but perfect love casts out fear. For fear has to do with punishment, and whoever fears has not been perfected in love. We love because he first loved us. If anyone says, "I love God," and hates his brother, he is a liar, for he who does not love his brother whom he has seen cannot love God whom he has not seen. And this commandment we have from him: whoever loves God must also love his brother. - 1 John 4:16,18-21

He had no form or majesty that we should look at him, and no beauty that we should desire him. He was despised and rejected by men; a man of sorrows, and acquainted with grief; and as one from whom men hide their faces he was despised, and we esteemed him not. Surely he has borne our griefs and carried our sorrows; yet we esteemed him stricken, smitten by God, and afflicted. But he was pierced for our transgressions; he was crushed for our iniquities; upon him was the chastisement that brought us peace, and with his wounds we are healed. - Isaiah 53:2b-5

Chapter 15

Rejoice always, pray without ceasing, give thanks in all circumstances; for this is the will of God in Christ Jesus for you. - 1 Thessalonians 5:16-18

Hope deferred makes the heart sick, but a desire fulfilled is a tree of life. - Proverbs 13:12

Notes

Chapter 1

1.   Lewis, C. S. The Weight of Glory and Other Addresses. William Collins, 2013.

Chapter 3

1.   Black, Christa. Heart Made Whole: Turning Your Unhealed Pain into Your Greatest Strength. Grand Rapids, MI: Zondervan, 2016. Print.

2.   Piper, John. Desiring God. Multnomah Books, 1996.

Chapter 4

1.   Saffles, Gretchen. Ruth: Gospel of Grace. Knoxville, TN: Well Watered Women, 2017. Print.

2.   Chandler, Lauren. Steadfast Love. B & H Books, 2016.

3.   Gunn, Robin Jones, and Tricia Goyer. Praying for Your Future Husband: Preparing Your Heart for His. Colorado Springs, CO: Multnomah, 2011. Print.

Chapter 5

1.   Shirer, Priscilla. The Armor of God, Bible Study Book: Priscilla Shirer

Chapter 6

1.   Ivey, Jamie. "The Happy Hour #112: Tara Leigh Cobble." Www.jamieivey.com, Jamie Ivey, 26 Oct. 2016, jamieivey.com/happy-hour-112-tara-leigh-cobble.

Chapter 7

1.	Stanley, Sandra. Comparison Trap: A 28- Day Devotional for Women. North Point Ministries, Inc., 2015. Print

2.	Milner, Rachael. "When Everything Is Not Enough." Well Watered Women Blog, 16 Feb. 2017, wellwateredwomen.com/blog/everything-is-not-enough-1?rq=jesus plus nothing.

Chapter 8

1.	Cloud, Henry. How to Get a Date Worth Keeping: Be Dating in Six Months or Your Money Back. Zondervan, 2005.

2.	www.trueidentityministries.org

3.	TerKeurst, Lysa. Uninvited: Living Loved When You Feel Less Than, Left Out, and Lonely. Nashville: Thomas Nelson, 2016. Print.

Chapter 9

1.	Saffles, Gretchen. A God-Sized Love Story: Beautiful Redemption From Beginning to End. 2013.

Chapter 12

1.	Arthur, Kay. Covenant Bible Study Book Gods Enduring Promises. Lifeway Christian Resources, 2009.

2.	Downs, Annie F. Looking for Lovely: Collecting the Moments That Matter. B & H Books, 2016.

Chapter 13

1.	Saffles, Gretchen. "Why I Won't Quit Social Media." www.wellwateredwomen.com, 12 July 2017, wellwateredwomen.com/blog/why-i-wont-quit-social-media.

Chapter 14

1.   Loechner, Erin. Chasing Slow: Courage to Journey off the Beaten Path. Zondervan, 2017.

2.   Moore, Beth. "James: Mercy Triumphs by Beth Moore." B&H Publishing Group.

Chapter 15

1.   The Cultivate Shop Powersheets

https://shop.cultivatewhatmatters.com/pages/2018-powersheets

Thank you so much for taking the time to read this book. It means so much to me! I would love to hear from you and connect with you. I would love to hear your story!

Connect with me through email at alreadychosenbook@gmail.com.

Follow along with my journey and say hi on Instagram at @jessicanmathisen.

If you enjoyed this book, it would mean the world to me if you shared it on your favorite social media platform using the hashtag #alreadychosenbook.

Grace and peace,

Jessica

Made in the USA
Columbia, SC
24 November 2020